understanding **empiricism**

Understanding Movements in Modern Thought
Series Editor: Jack Reynolds

This series provides short, accessible and lively introductions to the major schools, movements and traditions in philosophy and the history of ideas since the beginning of the Enlightenment. All books in the series are written for undergraduates meeting the subject for the first time.

Published

Understanding Empiricism
Robert G. Meyers

Understanding Existentialism
Jack Reynolds

Understanding Phenomenology
David R. Cerbone

Understanding Poststructuralism
James Williams

Understanding Virtue Ethics
Stan van Hooft

Forthcoming titles include

Understanding Ethics
Tim Chappell

Understanding Feminism
Peta Bowden and Jane Mummery

Understanding German Idealism
Will Dudley

Understanding Hegelianism
Robert Sinnerbrink

Understanding Hermeneutics
Lawrence Schmidt

Understanding Naturalism
Jack Ritchie

Understanding Rationalism
Charlie Heunemann

Understanding Utilitarianism
Tim Mulgan

understanding **empiricism**

Robert G. Meyers

ACUMEN

*For Rosalie,
with love*

First published in 2006 by Acumen

Acumen Publishing Limited
15a Lewins Yard
East Street
Chesham
Bucks HP5 1HQ
www.acumenpublishing.co.uk

ISBN-10: 1-84465-058-8   ISBN-13: 978-1-84465-058-3   (hardcover)
ISBN-10: 1-84465-059-6   ISBN-13: 978-1-84465-059-0   (paperback)

British Library Cataloguing-in-Publication Data
A catalogue record for this book is available from the British Library.

Designed and typeset by Kate Williams, Swansea.
Printed and bound in Malta by Gutenberg Press.

Contents

Abbreviations

Dialogue George Berkeley, *Principles of Human Knowledge and Three Dialogues*, R. Woolhouse (ed.) (Harmondsworth: Penguin, 1988). References in the text are to Dialogue number and page.

DNR David Hume, *Dialogues Concerning Natural Religion*, N. Kemp Smith (ed.) (Indianapolis, IN: Bobbs-Merrill, 1947). Referred to dialogue number and page.

EHU David Hume, *An Enquiry Concerning Human Understanding*, in *Enquiries*, 3rd ed., L. A. Selby-Bigge (ed.) (Oxford: Oxford University Press, 1975). References are to the section and page number.

Essay John Locke, *An Essay Concerning Human Understanding*, R. Woolhouse (ed.) (Harmondsworth: Penguin, 1997). References in the text are to the book, chapter and section, e.g. IV ii 14.

Examination J. S. Mill, *An Examination of Sir William Hamilton's Philosophy* (Toronto: University of Toronto Press, 1979).

Meditation René Descartes, *Meditations on First Philosophy,* in *Philosophical Essays and Correspondence*, R. Ariew (ed.) (Indianapolis, IN: Hackett, 2000). References are to the number of the Meditation, e.g. *Meditation* I, and page.

PHK George Berkeley, *Principles of Human Knowledge and Three Dialogues*, R. Woolhouse (ed.) (Harmondsworth: Penguin, 1988). References in the text are to section number.

Problems Bertrand Russell, *Problems of Philosophy* (Oxford: Oxford University Press, 1959).

System John Stuart Mill, *System of Logic* (London: Longman, 1959). Referred to in text by book, chapter, section and page.

Treatise David Hume, *A Treatise of Human Nature*, L. A. Selby-Bigge (ed.) (Oxford: Oxford University Press, 1988). Referred to as *Treatise* with book, chapter and section, e.g. I iv 2, and page.

introduction

Empiricism and rationalism

Every list of the great empiricists would include John Locke (1632–1704), George Berkeley (1685–1753) and David Hume (1711–1776), but many commentators argue that they do not agree on a doctrine we can call empiricism. But this is premature. There is a basic and important thesis they share. Locke states it clearly in a note about proofs of the existence of God. He says:

> Real existence can be proved only by real existence; and, therefore, the real existence of a God can only be proved by the real existence of other things. The real existence of other things without us can be evidenced to us only by our senses; but our own existence is known to us by a certainty yet higher than our senses give us of the existence of other things, and that is internal perception, self-consciousness, or intuition; from whence therefore may be drawn, by a train of ideas, the surest and most incontestable proof of a God. (Locke 1972: 316)

These remarks are a comment on René Descartes (1596–1650), who holds that God's existence can be proved from our concept of him. By definition he is a perfect being and, according to Descartes, the idea of perfection could only come from an actually perfect being. Locke claims that we cannot prove the existence of anything without appealing to experience. Real existence can be proved only by real existence and our only evidence for this is experience, that is, *external perception* of things oustide us and *internal perception* of our own existence and the workings of our minds. This is a clear expression of empiricism: all knowledge of real existence must be based on the senses or self-consciousness, that is, on experience. Locke's own argument for God meets this condition. He holds that we are conscious that we exist and are thinking beings and, since matter cannot explain thought, concludes that a thinking being created the material world. This is an empiricist argument, since it rests on premises that are (i) about real existents, as opposed to concepts, and (ii) are certified by experience. By 'real existence', Locke means existence independent of thought and by 'ideal existence' existence in the mind. Reasoning from ideal to real existence is never valid; to show that something is real we must experience it or infer it from something we experience.

This suggests that *rationalism* asserts that *some* claims to real existence can be justified independently of experience, or are *a priori*, to use the technical term, while *empiricism* holds that *no* such claims can be justified *a priori*. Empiricism can also be expressed as the view that *all* justification of beliefs about real existence is dependent on experience, or empirical.

A word should be said about real existence. For something to be real is for it to exist independently of what anyone thinks about it, or, as the scholastics put it, to exist independently of any intellectual consideration, while ideal existence is existence in thought alone. If I dream of having tea with the Mad Hatter and the Queen, the fact that I had the dream is real, but the object of the dream, the tea party, is not. It exists only in my mind and has only ideal existence. (This is the origin of the ordinary meaning of an ideal as a perfect state of things: ideals exist in thought until they are realized.) Similarly the Mad Hatter himself is an ideal existent, since he exists only as a fictional or imagined character, while the Queen is real.

This understanding of empiricism and rationalism centres on the justification of our beliefs. There is also an issue about the *origin of concepts*. Descartes argues that some ideas and knowledge are innate and hence not based on experience. The result is that Locke also has to argue that all ideas and beliefs are acquired by experience. There are thus two issues. The question of justification is about the sort of evidence required to warrant a proposition and is an epistemic question (a question about the quality of our evidence), while the question of the origin of concepts and beliefs is psychological. These are distinct issues. Beliefs do not have to be innate in order to be justified *a priori*. It might be that all concepts and beliefs are acquired through experience, perhaps because they involve language, but that some beliefs are justified *a priori*. Locke holds, for instance, that we know *a priori* that red is red even though the idea of red is not innate, but acquired by experience. On the other hand, the empiricist does not have to argue that all ideas are learned by experience to defend the claim that real-existence claims must be justified empirically. Similarly, although many traditional rationalists (Plato, Descartes and Leibniz) held that there are innate concepts, this is not essential to their thesis that some knowledge of reality is *a priori*.

To distinguish the questions of origin and justification, we can call the claim that beliefs about reality must be justified empirically *justificatory empiricism* and the thesis that all concepts and beliefs are acquired by experience *conceptual empiricism*. In the future, 'empiricism' and 'rationalism' without an adjective will refer to the justificatory senses. The conceptual doctrines will be referred to with the adjective, unless the context makes it clear that they are intended.

Several points should be noted about the justificatory issue. First, empiricism and rationalism are contradictory. One asserts that there is *some a priori* knowledge of reality and the other denies it. This means that one cannot be both an empiricist and rationalist at the same time. An empiricist might hold other doctrines usually associated with famous rationalists, but this does not make him a rationalist so long as he denies *a priori* knowledge of real existence.

Secondly, a rationalist need not hold that *all* knowledge of reality is *a priori*. This is an extreme thesis few rationalists have held. He is only committed to holding that at least one instance of such knowledge is *a priori*. This implies a related point. In denying that there is any *a priori* knowledge of reality, the empiricist makes a more general claim than the rationalist. He is committed to showing that *no* knowledge of existence is *a priori*, while the rationalist needs only one case to prove his position.

Thirdly, an empiricist need not deny the existence of *a priori* knowledge. He is only committed to holding that there is no *a priori* knowledge of real existence. He might claim, as Locke, Berkeley, Hume and most empiricists have, that there is *a priori* knowledge but hold that it is only

---

KEY POINT *Rationalism and empiricism*
- *Empiricism*: all knowledge of real existence must be justified by experience, that is, is empirical.
- *Rationalism*: some such knowledge is *a priori* or justified independently of experience.
- *Conceptual empiricism*: all concepts are acquired by experience.
- *Conceptual rationalism* (or innatism): some concepts are innate.

about the conceptual order and not about reality, that is, not about a realm of entities independent of what anyone might think about them. We shall discuss various empiricist theories of the *a priori* in Chapter 5.

Fourthly, empiricism and rationalism are about the *sources* of our knowledge of reality and are epistemological doctrines. They do not imply specific doctrines about what is real and are independent of metaphysical claims. This last point raises the question of the distinction between epistemology and metaphysics.

In general, epistemology deals with the nature and grounds of knowledge and its extent. It is a critique of evidence and so is an extension of logic. Questions of whether some things can be known and how they are known are epistemological while questions of the existence and nature of things, qualities and events are metaphysical (other than questions that are specifically epistemological, such as 'What is knowledge?' and 'Is there knowledge of *X*?'). This includes questions about the nature of mental attitudes and certain basic entities epistemologists frequently discuss. For example, the nature of belief, truth and the status of propositions and sense data (i.e. the objects of sensations) fall outside the theory of knowledge proper. The epistemologist accepts the existence of beliefs and propositions (at least nominally) and leaves the question of what they are to science and metaphysics. This does not mean that he does not have metaphysical views or that they do not influence his theory of knowledge, but only that they are not his main concern as an epistemologist. When he discusses the nature of belief or truth, he is straying from the theory of knowledge and getting into other issues, issues in the philosophy of mind, semantics or metaphysics (and perhaps even psychology).

This has an important implication for empiricism and rationalism. An empiricist might or might not hold that God exists. What he is committed to as an empiricist, as we saw in the passage from Locke, is that we can know that he exists only on the basis of experience; he cannot hold that we can know it on *a priori* grounds. He might go on to argue that there are good empirical arguments for his existence or deny that there are. But this is a further issue and concerns his views on the quality of the empirical evidence for God's existence: epistemic views, to be sure, but ones that are independent of his acceptance of empiricism. Empiricism only restricts him to the sort of evidence that might be offered to show that God exists; it makes no claim whether there is or is not such evidence.

These remarks show that empiricism may be worked out in many different ways. Empiricists argue that there is no *a priori* knowledge of reality, but this does not commit them to agreement on other issues. As a result, it is difficult to make significant generalizations from empiricism to other philosophic doctrines. Locke holds that God exists and is a realist about physical objects while Berkeley agrees with him about God but holds that physical objects are dependent on mind and Hume is skeptical about God and at times about the physical world as well.

Empiricism and rationalism are sometimes defined in terms of analytic and synthetic propositions. This terminology derives from Immanuel Kant (1724–1804). He holds that the truth of an analytic proposition depends solely on its meaning while synthetic propositions go beyond this. 'Unicorns are one-horned creatures' is analytic while 'Unicorns come to the aid of maidens in distress' is synthetic. Unicorns must have a single horn but they are not by definition protectors of virgins (although this is part of their legend). Kant holds that all analytic propositions can be known *a priori* and that, while many synthetic ones are empirical, there are also synthetic *a priori* propositions. This has led many twentieth-century writers to define 'rationalism' as the claim that there is synthetic *a priori* knowledge and 'empiricism' as the thesis that there is no synthetic *a priori*.

The defect with this as a definition of 'empiricism' is that it leaves out one of the main claims made by rationalists. Descartes, Spinoza and Leibniz hold that 'God exists' is true since God is the most perfect conceivable being by definition and so must exist. This makes 'God exists' analytic by Kant's criterion, but, according to Kant, analytic propositions are purely conceptual and do not imply existence; every true proposition of the form '*X* exists' is synthetic. This implies that the rationalists' claim that God can be known to exist from our concept of him is contradictory; 'God exists' cannot be both analytic and imply existence. Some people are happy to accept this, but the more reasonable conclusion is that this definition of rationalism begs the question against them. Explications of philosophic terms should not rule out major positions by definition, but provide a neutral framework for discussing the issues. (One might amend Kant's definitions and drop the requirement that existence claims cannot be analytic, but this easily leads to confusion since the term 'analytic' is so firmly entrenched.)

One must also be careful of empiricists who combine their denial of *a priori* knowledge of real existence with other doctrines, then claim that theirs is the only form of empiricism. Such empiricists are similar to prophets who claim that those who disagree with them are apostates. As an abstract thesis, 'empiricism' may be conjoined with other theses, but generically all empiricists are the same. If *E* is the thesis that there is no *a priori* knowledge of reality, *E* may be conjoined with other claims to make a version of empiricism, but any conjunction that accepts *E* accepts empiricism. To hold that empiricism or "true empiricism" is the conjunction of *E* with some other thesis *p* may be termed *conjunctivitis* (since it prevents its defenders from seeing things clearly).

An example of this is logical positivism, which flourished in the mid-twentieth century. The main figures in this movement were Moritz Schlick, Rudolf Carnap and Hans Reichenbach. They held three theses: (i) all knowledge of reality is empirical; (ii) all *a priori* knowledge (including logic and mathematics) is analytic and hence not about reality; and (iii) metaphysics is meaningless in the sense that its claims are neither true nor false, since metaphysical propositions cannot be verified by sense experience. The first thesis made them empiricists, and the second made them *logical* empiricists since they conceded that logical knowledge is *a priori*, but not about reality. The third thesis was their most distinctive doctrine and may be called *verificationism*.

This is clearly a version of empiricism, but it is a mistake to take it as the only version. Many thinkers we recognize as empiricists have held unverifiable metaphysical theories (e.g. Locke and Hume). To build the rejection of metaphysics into empiricism thus clouds the issue. It also led some rationalists to think they were refuting empiricism in the traditional sense when they attacked the positivists' verificationism. Philosophic definitions should reflect the central issues in the debates. Building in other issues only confuses them. (Another example of conjunctivitis: 'realism' about physical objects is sometimes defined as the doctrine that (i) there are physical objects independent of thought and (ii) we can have knowledge about them, then rejected on the ground that (ii) is false, even though the basic meaning of "realism" in this context is (i) alone.)

Another mistake is to take philosophers whose general outlook is sympathetic to Locke and Hume to be empiricists even though they accept *a priori* knowledge of a real conceptual realm. An example is the early Bertrand Russell. In 1912, he agreed with the empiricists that all knowledge of "existence" is based on experience, but held that we also have *a priori* knowledge of a "realm of being" that does not exist, but subsists (Russell 1959: 73–5, 99–100). Existence in his sense includes physical objects and spirits (if there are any) that exist in space and time, while subsistence includes abstract entities such as universals and relations. (Note that it is not clear where he places God, who is neither spatial nor abstract.) This has led some to think that he is an empiricist, but he is not according to the account given here. Even though subsistent entities do not exist in his sense, he holds that they "have being" independently of what we think about them *and* that we have *a priori* knowledge of them. He is thus committed to *a priori* knowledge of reality, and is a rationalist despite his other views. It is also important to note that this is not just because he recognizes a realm of reality beyond the spatial–temporal sphere. A Platonic world is consistent with empiricism, so long as we deny that our knowledge of it is *a priori*. (We shall see that Locke thought the basic laws of nature might be necessary truths, as rationalists do, while denying that we can have *a priori* knowledge of it.)

We will consider Locke's criticism of innatism and his defence of both forms of empiricism in Chapter 1. Chapters 2 and 3 will deal with Berkeley and Hume respectively. Later chapters will discuss problems that arise from empiricism: the question of foundations versus coherence, the *a priori* and the charge that it leads to skepticism. Chapter 7 discusses some of the ways in which empiricism influences religious belief.

one

Locke, knowledge and the innate

The first and perhaps greatest classic of modern empiricism is John Locke's *Essay Concerning Human Understanding* (1690). The work is divided into four books. The first criticizes innate knowledge, the second explains the origin of ideas in experience, the third discusses language and the fourth the nature and extent of knowledge. The result is an extended discussion of both versions of empiricism. In this chapter, we will focus on his defence of conceptual empiricism and his conception of scientific knowledge and its limits. Other aspects of his theory will be considered in Chapter 2 in connection with Berkeley's criticisms in Chapter 2.

Locke on innate knowledge

Locke's criticism of innate ideas and knowledge is part of his general theory of scientific knowledge. He opposed Descartes's rationalist theory and the Aristotelian-medieval theory. Among the examples of innate truths he considers are:

(1) Whatever is, is.
(2) It is impossible for the same thing to be and not to be.
(3) Do as one would be done to.
(4) Virtue is the best worship of God.
(5) God exists.

Locke's discussion is divided into three parts. First, he attacks the claim that there are innate speculative truths such as (1) and (2). He rejects Descartes's claim that these are general maxims presupposed by all knowledge and so unlearned. Locke holds that we can have knowledge without knowing general propositions such as (1) and (2) and hence do not have to posit them as innate. Secondly, he considers the case for innate practical or moral principles such as (3) and (4). He argues that it is always reasonable to ask for a reason for a moral claim. Even (3) (the "golden rule") is not seen to be true as soon as it is understood (like 'Blue is not red', which Locke holds is self-evident). One might understand the rule, yet still ask for a reason why it should be believed. As a result, the claim that all innate moral truths are self-evident and need no reason is false. Thirdly, he argues that a belief cannot be innate unless its ideas are also innate, but that the ideas in standard examples (such as (5), 'God exists') are not innate, but acquired. His general conclusions are: (a) innatism is unfounded, since we can explain all our ideas on the basis of experience; (b) the criteria for innate knowledge and the notion itself are hopelessly unclear; and (c) this unclarity can only lead to dogmatism. He says that once men found principles they could not doubt, it was "a short and easy way to conclude them innate". This eased "the lazy from the pains of search" and stopped enquiry into "all that was once styled innate" (*Essay*: I iv 24). Knowledge depends "upon the right use of those powers nature has bestowed upon us" and not on inborn principles or on what other men know. We may as easily "hope to see with other men's eyes, as to know by other men's understandings". "Such borrowed wealth, like fairy-money, though it were gold in the hand from which he received it, will be but leaves and dust when it comes to use" (I iv 22, 23).

Critics sometimes argue that he does not prove in each case that the principles (or their ideas) are not innate, but he never claims to be able to prove this. He says he is offering an alternative and more plausible theory of the origin of our ideas (and hence knowledge). So long as this theory is not demonstrated to be false by the proponents of innateness, they have not proved their case, but have only shown that it is a possible account of the matter.

I shall concentrate on Locke's criticism of innate speculative truths. His main target is Descartes, who held that innatism is necessary to defend the reality of scientific knowledge, but both their theories have their roots in the medieval theory of science. Let us first look at this medieval theory.

Following Aristotle, the scholastics held that all ideas derive from experience or, as Thomas Aquinas (1224–1274) put it, "There is nothing in the understanding that was not previously in the senses" (Copleston 1952: 393). They held that the world of nature contains objects with form and matter; when we perceive them, we become aware of the forms without the matter, which then become the materials of our knowledge. We can be assured that this knowledge is genuine since there is a correspondence between the forms in our minds and the forms in reality. The view may be summarized in three theses.

(i) Perception is the reception of the form of an object without its matter. Physical objects differ in their form and exist because this form is instantiated in matter. A rose, for instance, is matter with a colour and shape that distinguishes it from a lilac or a rabbit. When we perceive it, we are aware of these distinguishing characteristics without the matter.

(ii) By abstracting some of the qualities of the object from others, we acquire new concepts, such as the concepts of red, petals, flower and even the more general concept of a plant. All simple concepts are acquired by a similar process. Then, by combining these abstract ideas, we form complex ideas of objects we have not experienced, such as the idea of God and of things that do not exist at all, for example, the ideas of unicorns and centaurs.

(iii) The basic ideas, however, such as the ideas of a rose, a horse and a man, correspond to features in the objects. The result is that perception gives us adequate ideas of natural objects and their species. By further comparison and generalization, we arrive at general principles and ultimately laws of nature and science. Since the ideas derive from the transference of forms in nature to the mind, we can be assured that there is a correspondence between them and nature, and that our science is genuine.

We may call (i) the *reception thesis*, (ii) the *abstraction thesis* and (iii) the *correspondence thesis*.

This Aristotelian theory was accepted in its broad outlines for almost two thousand years until the new science of the seventeenth century called it into question. This "new science" was actually an extension of ancient atomism, which held that objects are not composed of a material and a formal element, but of insensible particles in motion. The colour and shape of a rose are a result of a certain configuration of particles or corpuscles (which we would now term atoms and molecules), which are themselves neither roses nor red. Descartes accepted this, although he rejected the ancient atomists' theory that things are composed of void or empty space as well as particles. He thought every part of space is filled with particles that move together somewhat the way in which oil moves in water when it is stirred. But he agreed with most of the scientists at the time that physical objects are systems of insensible particles rather than substantial entities composed of matter and form. As a result, he rejected the reception theory of perception. Perception occurs when corpuscles from the object strike the senses, causing particles in the body to move until an image is formed in the mind. Perception is not the transference of a form from object to mind, but occurs by impulse. Furthermore, the picture we have of the world with its shapes and colours and apparently solid objects is mistaken; it is actually composed of colourless extended particles in motion (which are always in touch with other particles, since there is no vacuum). The world is not as it appears, but radically different.

In explaining this theory, Descartes compares perceptual ideas to words. Just as words do not resemble the qualities they represent, so ideas do not resemble their objects. They are signs that signal their presence and lead us to avoid or pursue them. But as resemblances they are "false". He also compares us to blind men who use a cane. There is no more resemblance between our ideas and reality than there is between the blind man's sensations of the end of his cane and reality. This led him to conclude that if we are to have an adequate scientific conception of the world, the senses cannot be trusted as the source of our concepts, so he rejected the abstraction thesis as well. To save the reality of knowledge, he holds that geometrical and scientific concepts (as well as metaphysical concepts such as the ideas of substance and God) do not arise from experience, but are innate. And, since he can prove *a priori* that God exists and is good, we can be assured that these ideas are adequate and correspond to the world. The result is that even though he rejects the reception thesis, Descartes still accepts the correspondence thesis, but at the expense of the abstraction thesis. Concepts such as those of triangularity, extension, substance, infinity and even of God are not derived from experience, but are part of the mind's native equipment. But he does not go so far as to argue that all knowledge is innate. He thinks perception can be trusted if it is carefully examined in the light of innate ideas and the principles based on them, and after we have validated its reliability by appeal to God's will. The result is a science of reality based in part on experience, but ultimately certified on the basis of innate ideas and *a priori* proofs.

Locke agrees that the Aristotelian–scholastic theory of perception is mistaken. Simple ideas like those of the sweetness and whiteness of sugar do not resemble qualities in sugar; at best they are caused by powers in it to produce them, but this is only a minimal correspondence. Unlike Descartes, however, he continues to accept abstraction as the source of ideas. Our ideas may or may not correspond to external objects, but we can know this only by appealing to experience. Locke, in other words, rejects the reception thesis, but accepts the abstraction thesis, and accepts the correspondence thesis only in severely modified form. Nothing in our ideas guarantees that they correspond with reality, since abstraction is a selective process and may lead us astray.

This might seem a reasonable alternative to the scholastic theory, but it has a troubling aspect. Descartes argues that innateness will allow our scientific conclusions to be known with certainty, but Locke is forced to give this up. This means that the medieval sense of science as absolute certainty must give way to probability and analogical reasoning, and since Locke continues to hold that knowledge must be certain, this implies that there is no scientific knowledge. This skeptical conclusion did not bother Locke or many of his contemporaries, but it has worried others. We shall say more about it in § "Nominal and real essences" (p. 26).

Locke offers several arguments against innateness:

- He argues that no truths are universally accepted as we would expect if they were innate in all human beings. Many people do not have a European conception of God, and children and idiots have none at all. Children and primitive peoples also do not seem to have highly abstract ideas such as those of identity and infinity, even though these are thought to be the most basic innate ideas of all. (He gives similar arguments against innate practical or moral principles.) Furthermore, even if there were universally accepted principles, this would not prove them innate, since they and their ideas might be acquired by common experience.
- Defenders of innatism have an answer to this. They hold that these principles are still in their minds *potentially*; people who do not seem to have the necessary innate ideas on which they are based have not reflected sufficiently to become aware of them. Locke argues that if this is the case all knowledge is innate, since in order to know something we must have an innate power to become aware of it. Potentiality of awareness is not enough to show that there is innate knowledge. We shall return to this shortly.
- Locke also argues that in order to know that a proposition is true we must have perceived it to be true at some time in the past, where 'perception' is taken to imply apprehension or awareness.

This implies that at some time prior to birth, we must have been aware of their truth and Locke takes this to be most implausible.

- His main argument is that we do not have to accept innatism in order to explain our ideas. They can be explained by abstraction. The idea of God, for instance, is a complex idea of a thinking substance who is perfect and infinitely powerful, and each of these simpler ideas can be traced back to the perception of external objects ("outer sense") and the perception of our own minds and its contents ("inner sense").

Several features of Locke's position are often overlooked. First, he claims not to offer "undeniable cogent demonstrations" of his theory, as Descartes did, but "to *appeal* to men's own unprejudiced *experience*, and observation" whether his principles are acceptable. He hopes it will be "an edifice uniform" and that he will not have "to shore it up with props and buttresses, leaning on borrowed or begged foundations; or at least, if mine prove a castle in the air, I will endeavour it shall be of a piece, and hang together" (*Essay*: I iv 25). He develops his alternative theory in Book II by showing in detail how our ideas can be explained on the basis of experience alone.

This leaves room for Descartes's theory, since Locke does not claim to prove that innatism is false, but it still puts the Cartesian in a difficult position. Descartes claims that his theory can be shown to be true with certainty. By showing that there is an alternative theory, Locke puts the innatist in the position of having to prove with certainty that his alternative is unacceptable, since a theory or belief cannot be proved with certainty so long as there is a possible (i.e. consistent) alternative. Furthermore, the Cartesian must prove that it is false without appealing to innatism itself, since this would beg the question. The only other option is to argue that innatism is the more plausible theory to account for the facts and Locke thinks most people will accept his empiricist theory on this ground.

One way to put his view is that he holds that empiricism with abstraction is the more reasonable hypothesis. If a phenomenon can be explained by more than one theory, we cannot prove one over the other with certainty unless we can prove that the other accounts are false. Locke holds that, since there is no direct proof of innatism and empiricism cannot be disproved, the best we can do is to accept the more plausible account, which he thinks is the empiricist one.

Secondly, Locke argues that learning ideas such as those of substance, identity and God requires a great deal of time and depends on learning a language as well. A child may know that "an apple is not fire" because it has the concepts of fire and apple from experience, but it will take years before it will assent to principles such as (2), that is, that it is impossible for the same thing to be and not be at the same time. He might learn the words, but Locke says their meanings are so "large, comprehensive, and abstract" that it will take a great deal longer before he learns their precise meanings and understands the principle itself (*Essay*: I ii 23).

This too is often overlooked. Descartes's only argument for innate ideas is that we do not find ideas such as substance and power when we examine external objects, but he restricts his enquiry to what he is aware of at the moment. He gives several examples. One is that we have two ideas of the sun. The senses tell us that it is a small disc in the sky while the intellect tells us that it is "several times larger than the earth". These cannot both resemble the real sun and reason tells him that the intellectual idea is to be preferred, since it is derived from astronomical reasoning and "is elicited from certain notions that are innate in me" (*Meditation* III: 115). But this is far from decisive. The intellectual idea can also be derived from experience if we consider its influence over time, as Locke suggests. Similar remarks apply to Descartes's example of the piece of the wax (in *Mediation* II: 111). His senses tell him that the wax is solid, cool and has a certain shape at one time, and is soft, warm and has another shape at another, even though he knows that the wax is "extended, flexible, and mutable". He also knows that it is the same piece of wax at both times despite the fact that all of its sensory qualities are different. He concludes that he cannot know these truths by the senses, but must know them by "an inspection on the part of the mind alone".

In both cases, Descartes assumes too narrow a view of the effects of experience. According to Locke, astronomy and knowledge of objects such as the wax are based solely on ideas derived from experience considered over time. To try to settle the issue by reducing the senses to what we can know at a given moment distorts the empiricist's view. We start with rudimentary experience, then learn language, distinctions and generalizations from experience, and come to knowledge and a sophisticated understanding of things only much later.

As these remarks indicate, the debate is complicated and involves a series of assertions and counter-assertions. What is the central issue? The answer is that Descartes and Locke have two different conceptions of our innate powers to have knowledge. They agree that knowledge requires innate potentialities, but disagree on the role experience plays in bringing this knowledge to consciousness. An example might prove useful. A child has an innate capacity to play chess, but he does not have the ability to play it until he matures and learns the rules of the game, that is, he needs experience in order to bring his capacity to actuality. He also has an innate capacity to crave sugar, but this is different from his capacity to play chess. In the case of chess, experience plays a formative role in channelling the capacity, while in the case of sugar his desire is activated as soon as he tastes it. Experience is necessary to structure the innate power to play chess in a certain direction, while the desire for sweets only needs experience to trigger it. We may say that an innate *capacity* is a potentiality that needs structuring by experience before it can operate, whereas an innate *ability* is already structured at birth and only needs experience to trigger it.

Descartes holds that innate knowledge is not a bare potentiality, but is fully formed at birth; the only role of experience is to bring it to consciousness. Locke thinks that experience does not merely trigger our capacity for knowledge, but is needed to shape it. In scholastic terminology, innatists hold that experience is only the *occasion* or *proximate cause* of knowledge already fully formed in the mind, while Locke holds that it is the formative or *remote cause* of it. The debate is not about knowledge, but about the nature of the mind. The rationalists take the intellect to be a separate faculty (or substance) housed in the body with fully formed abilities that rely on ideas from experience only incidentally. As the medievals put it, it is a gift of God given to us by a special creation and is not the result of an interaction between nature and innate capacities that we share with other animals. This is a metaphysical issue and not a specifically epistemological one. Locke's interest in it is partly metaphysical and partly epistemological. He wants to defend a more naturalistic account of the intellect and also accepts the empiricist's theory that experience is the only source of knowledge of reality. He holds that our innate potentiality for knowledge and ideas is a capacity that needs to be shaped by experience.

That this is the issue is clearer in Leibniz's criticism of Locke than it is in Descartes's. Leibniz offered several arguments against Locke that have become famous, but they are of uneven quality. One centres on Locke's remark that the mind at birth is a *tabula rasa* or blank tablet on which experience writes (his actual words are "white paper, void of all characters"; *Essay*: I i 2). Locke mentions this in passing as a metaphor to explain his theory, but Leibniz treats it as a central argument. He says the mind is not a blank tablet at birth, but is more like a block of marble with veins in it. Experience writes on it but only along certain innate lines. Virtually every modern discussion of the debate repeats these metaphors, but they show very little. At most, they point up Leibniz's view that the mind is already structured at birth. But this only illustrates one of the issues between him and Locke. It also distorts the main issue. Locke holds that we have innate powers as much as Leibniz, so the marble metaphor fits him as much as Leibniz. He denies that it has ideas, beliefs and knowledge at birth, so it is blank with respect to them, but he does not hold that we have no innate cognitive capacities. He would agree that the tablet has veins, but deny that some of them represent innate *knowledge* and *ideas*.

Leibniz also misconstrues Locke's account of experience. He says that Locke holds that all ideas derive from sensation and downplays his explicit claim that they derive from experience in the broad sense that includes reflection. *Outer sense* is external perception and is the source of our ideas of physical objects and their qualities, while *inner sense* is introspection and is the source of our ideas of pain, anger, belief, memory, abstraction and the self, that is, of our emotions, mental states and ourselves. When Leibniz takes notice of Locke's recognition of reflection, he replies with a rhetorical question. If we allow this, he asks, can we deny that "there is a great deal that is innate in our minds, since we are innate to ourselves, so to speak, and since there is in ourselves Being, Unity, Substance, Duration, Change, Action, Perception, Pleasure, and hosts of other objects of our intellectual ideas?" (Leibniz 1981: 51–2). This, however, confuses the claim that the mind is a unified substance that endures with the claim that we have innate *ideas* of unity, substance and duration. Locke does not deny the first, but he denies that the ideas of these qualities of the mind are innate. We acquire them when we first reflect on ourselves and this is a species of experience. Leibniz is either confused or is using rhetoric (and distortion) to gain his point. Squirrels are also unified and enduring substances, but this alone does not show that they have innate ideas of unity, duration and substance. In his haste to refute Locke, he just passes over this.

He also overlooks Locke's claim that most knowledge is habitual or potential and is not always directly present to the mind. Locke holds that all knowledge except what we are currently thinking about is habitual; further, habitual knowledge requires actual perception of a truth, which in turn requires that we have the ideas from experience (*Essay*: IV i 8–9). For example, in order to know a theorem of geometry, a student must acquire the ideas and see that the theorem is true; the belief is then stored in memory and brought to mind at the time of the test and hopefully remains there as a habit for the rest of his life. Leibniz takes Locke's official view to be that nothing is potential in the mind and that the theory of habitual knowledge is an afterthought, but this is a mistake. Locke holds that first there is an innate capacity for knowledge, then ideas and perception of their relations, then habitual knowledge, which is stored in memory.

Leibniz's most interesting argument is that Locke cannot explain our knowledge of necessary truths. He says that experience cannot prove the necessity of common notions such as "Whatever is, is" and "Nothing can have a quality and not have it at the same time", no matter how extensive the confirming instances. He concludes that necessary truths such as those in geometry and arithmetic "must have principles whose proof does not depend on instances nor, consequently, on the testimony of the senses, even though without the senses it would never occur to us to think of them" (Leibniz 1981: 49–50).

This account of necessary truths runs together several questions Locke wants to distinguish. First, Locke agrees that mathematical truths are not generalizations from experience, but are known *a priori* (although he does not use the word). We know that $1 + 1 = 2$ as soon as we have the concepts of two, one, plus and identity, but these are acquired by experience and are not innate. Leibniz misses what is perhaps Locke's central point, namely, that the *origin* of our ideas and the *justification* of the propositions that contain them are independent questions and should not be confused. Locke agrees that mathematical and other necessary truths are justified independently of experience, and that our ability to know them is an innate capacity. What he denies is that the ideas that constitute them are innate; they are learned and we come to know necessary truths by reflecting on them. Despite his careful reading of Locke's *Essay*, Leibniz misses these subtleties. Locke also disagrees with the rationalists on a second thesis. He holds that necessary truths in mathematics are based on convention and that knowledge of them is not knowledge of real existence. We will look at his view on this second question in § "Nominal and real essences" (p. 26) and in more detail in Chapter 5.

Historically Locke's attack on innateness was devastating. Leibniz's *New Essays on Human Understanding* appeared long after they were both dead and did not diminish its influence in Britain or France. Locke's claim that concepts are acquired by experience became the established orthodoxy and the foundation for the development of psychology in the nineteenth and twentieth centuries.

Locke's new way of ideas

Locke's positive theory is that all ideas are based on simple ideas derived from experience. A simple idea is "in itself uncompounded and contains in it nothing but *one uniform appearance*, or conception in the mind, and is not distinguishable into different ideas" (*Essay*: II ii 1). The coldness and hardness we feel in a piece of ice are simple ideas, as are the ideas of white, sweet and solidity. These derive from external perception by means of the senses. We also have simple ideas that derive from reflection on our mental states. The ideas of pain, belief and the self are ideas of reflection.

The mind is passive in receiving these ideas: we cannot help but feel pain when we stub our foot or see the stone when we look at it. But we also have the ability to extend our ideas. First we can separate simple ideas from other ideas and form abstract ideas; secondly, we can combine them to make complex ideas, and thirdly, we can compare ideas to form ideas of relations. Let us look at these more closely.

- *Abstract ideas.* Locke spends most of the time discussing complex ideas, but the more basic operation is abstraction. He explains this as follows:

  > The senses at first let in particular ideas, and furnish the yet empty cabinet: and the mind by degrees growing familiar with some of them, they are lodged in the memory, and names got to them. Afterwards the mind proceeding further, abstracts them, and by degrees learns the use of general names.
  >
  > (*Essay*: I iv 15)

  Particular ideas of sensation are concrete images impressed on the senses, for example, the particular shade of red a child has when it sees a red apple or the image of its mother when she leans over its crib. These are "precise, naked appearances". By separating them from all other "circumstances of real existence, such as time, place or any other concomitant ideas", the mind creates abstract general ideas:

  > the same colour being observed today in chalk or snow, which the mind yesterday received from milk, it considers that appearance alone, makes it a representative of all of that kind; and having given it the name *whiteness*, it by that sound signifies the same quality wheresoever to be imagined or met with; and thus universals, whether ideas or terms, are made.
  >
  > (*Essay*: II xi 9)

- *Complex ideas.* These are often derived from experience, as when we perceive a house and have the particular idea of its shape, the arrangement of its windows and its colour, as well as the surrounding foliage. They can also be formed from simpler ideas. The idea of lead is the idea of a heavy, grayish white metal that is easily scratched. Ideas of fabulous creatures are formed from simple ideas, for example, the idea of a centaur with the torso of a man and the body of a horse, or of a mermaid with the torso of a woman and the body of a fish. The idea of God is also complex. Our idea of him is "a complex one of existence, knowledge, power, happiness, *etc*. infinite and eternal: which are all distinct ideas, and some of them being relative, are again compounded of others; all which being, as has been shown, originally got from *sensation* and *reflection*" (*Essay*: II xxiii 35).

- *Ideas of relation.* Ideas of relation are formed by comparing ideas. We bring two ideas together "to take a view of them at once, without uniting them into one". In this way we form the ideas of being greater than (as a whole is greater than the part) and of a mother as a parent of a child.

We thus have three contrasts: particular and abstract ideas; simple and complex ideas; relative and non-relative (or absolute) ideas. It is important to note that these classifications are not exclusive. Simple ideas can be particular or abstract (e.g. the simple idea of the chalk's whiteness when we see it is particular while the general idea of whiteness that applies to chalk and milk is abstract). Ideas of relation can also be simple or complex, particular or abstract. The idea of being a parent can be taken to be simple while the idea of being a mother is complex, consisting of the ideas of being a parent and being female.

In Book II of the *Essay*, Locke explains how various ideas might have derived from experience. The main classification is of complex ideas (*Essay*: II xii–xxiv). These can be of simple modes, mixed modes or substances. A simple mode is a modification or iteration of a simple idea. The ideas of space, time and number are simple-mode ideas: spatial ideas are modes of extension, temporal ideas modes of duration and numbers reiterations of the idea of unity. The idea of infinity is also a simple mode: places or moments iterated without end. Mixed-mode ideas are complexes of different kinds of simple ideas. Examples are the ideas of obligation and drunkenness. These may be derived from an original, as when we see a drunken man, but they are often put together without regard to whether anything real corresponds to them. Furthermore, they are not marks of "real beings that have a steady existence, but scattered and independent ideas, put together by the mind" (*Essay*:

II xxii 1). A murder, for example, does not exist through time, but takes place at a specific time. In this, mixed modes differ from substances. Ideas of substances contain ideas that "go constantly together". The idea of a horse contains the ideas of an animal having a characteristic shape, four legs, a mane and a long tail and, since we do not think these qualities can exist by themselves, the idea of a substratum "wherein they do subsist, and from which they do result" and which explains its existence through a length of time (*Essay*: II xxiii 1).

The details of this theory have been extensively criticized since Locke's day. In Chapter 2, we shall consider Berkeley's criticisms of abstraction, the notion of substance and Locke's theory that physical objects have primary and secondary qualities. The point at present is that the theory as a whole aims to show how we can acquire the different kinds of ideas from experience without postulating innate ideas: an alternative theory to innatism. He admits that his theory rests on certain assumptions, but argues that this is unavoidable when dealing with controversial issues. As we saw, the most he claims is that if it is "a castle in the air", at least it will be "all of a piece, and hang together" (*Essay*: I iv 25).

Knowledge and real existence

Locke defines knowledge as the perception of the agreement or disagreement of ideas. By an "agreement of ideas" he means an affirmative proposition and by a disagreement a negative proposition, for example, 'Apples are red' and 'Apples are not blue'. Identity and relational propositions ('Red is red' and 'Triangles between parallels with a common base are equal') can be known *a priori*, since they do not imply existence. Red is red even if nothing is red, and geometric propositions are true even if there are no triangles, circles or lines. He also holds that knowledge must be absolutely certain, although he hedges on this in the case of propositions about external physical objects, as we shall see.

The highest grade of knowledge is *intuition*, in which the mind perceives the truth as the eye perceives something in bright sunshine (*Essay*: IV ii 1). An example is 'Blue is not yellow'. As soon as we have the ideas of blue and yellow, and understand the words, we know that this is true. It is self-evident, that is, we know it to be true as soon as we understand it. The next grade is *demonstration*, which consists in proving a proposition from intuited premises by intuited steps. An example is 'The internal angles of a triangle equal two right angles'. This model fits mathematics, which Locke takes to be the most perfect knowledge we have. Mathematics is also *a priori* since it rests on abstraction and the definitions of the basic concepts (identity, addition, subtraction and the integers in arithmetic and line, triangle, circle in geometry). But this does not show that empiricism is false, since geometrical figures are abstract ideas and have "barely an *ideal existence*" in our minds; they are "fictions and contrivances of the mind" and do not apply real existence (*Essay*: IV iv 6).

Locke makes a sharp distinction between knowledge of universal propositions ('Every *S* is *P*') and knowledge of propositions about particulars (e.g. 'This is *S*' or 'Something is *S*'). Universal propositions depend on their ideas alone and do not imply the real existence of *S*. 'A triangle is a three-sided figure' and 'A centaur is half horse' are equally certain, but only because they are about ideal existence and do not depend on the existence of triangles or centaurs. Particular propositions, which are about real existence, are only known empirically. This implies that geometry is not about real space when taken as a demonstrative science. In order for it to apply to reality, we have to know that such things as straight lines and triangles are real, and this can only be justified empirically.

Propositions of real existence contain the idea of existence. To know that tigers exist is to perceive the agreement of the idea of tigers and the idea of real existence. Locke claims that we know the truth of three kinds of such propositions: that I exist is known to be true by intuition and 'God is' is known by demonstration. Propositions about external objects in one's immediate vicinity can be known by what he calls *sensitive knowledge*. Let us consider these in turn.

- *'I exist'*. Locke follows Descartes in holding that each of us knows that he exists. In thinking anything at all (even when doubting that we exist), we know that we exist, since thinking cannot occur unless there is a subject thinking. This is intuitive knowledge. We do not infer that we exist from the fact that we are thinking, but perceive it immediately in the act of thinking.

  Like all intuitive knowledge, this is absolutely certain, but Locke thinks it is also severely limited. First, a thinker can know that he exists only at the moment when he is thinking. That he existed a moment ago is not known with certainty, but is based on memory (although of course with an extremely high probability). Secondly, beyond knowing that he is a thinking being, he cannot know anything about his nature; in particular, he cannot know that he is a spiritual substance. On the first of these Locke agrees with Descartes. Descartes says that, no matter how much he doubts, he knows that he exists "is necessarily true every time that I utter it or conceive in my mind" (*Meditation* II: 108). But the second qualification is a departure from Descartes. Descartes holds that he not only knows that he exists, but that he is a immaterial spiritual substance as well. Locke makes no such claim. He holds that he may well be a thinking *material* substance. His reason is that he thinks that thinking matter is not a contradiction. Hence, from the fact that he is a thinking being, he cannot know intuitively that he is a mind as opposed to a material thing. He also cannot deduce that he is immaterial from his existence as a thinking being (see *Essay*: IV iii 6).

There is also a third difference. Descartes does not consider reflection (Locke's inner sense) to be experience, and so thinks that his knowledge that he exists is independent of experience, while Locke considers reflection to be as much a part of experience as sensation and external perception. Hence our knowledge that we exist is empirical and does not compromise his empiricism.

- '*God exists*'. Locke holds that our knowledge that God exists is an inference from our knowledge that we exist and so is demonstrative knowledge. His argument is this. (1) From our knowledge that we exist, we know that there must be something from eternity, since something cannot come from nothing. (2) We also know that "*this eternal being must be also the most powerful*", since all the powers we have must be "received from the same source". (3) This being must also be "*a knowing being from eternity*", since it is impossible that "things wholly void of knowledge, and operating blindly" could produce beings that have knowledge (*Essay*: IV x 3–5). Therefore there must be a knowing, immaterial being of great power that is eternal.

This is an empirical argument since it rests on the empirical premise that we exist and are thinking beings. It might be argued that step (3) is inconsistent with Locke's claim that it is possible for matter to think, but he has a reply to this. He does not think a configuration of material particulars can produce a thinking being *by itself*, but that it would be possible for God to make matter think since he can do anything that is not contradictory and is himself a thinking being. A world in which there was nothing but matter and no God could not have thinking beings, but God can make material things think by superadding the power of thought to them. What we know from the fact that we are thinking beings is that there is an eternal and immaterial being with the power (i) to create material objects and (ii) to give some of them the superadded power of thought. The possibility of thinking matter depends on a thinking God.

A more serious problem is that Locke may be taking too narrow a view of matter in arguing that no configuration of material particles can account for thought. His argument is based on the mechanistic understanding of matter of the seventeenth century. This held that particles are colourless solid balls somewhat like minuscule billiard balls in movement whose only interaction is through contact and impulse. It is difficult to understand how these could explain thought and perception. But it is not clear that it cannot be fully explained given the more complicated picture of the microscopic world dominant today. If it is logically possible for parcels of matter to think on their own without a superior thinking being adding thought to it, Locke's argument fails to prove that God exists. But this is a question of science and metaphysics, and not of epistemology.

- *Sensitive knowledge.* Locke's third degree of knowledge is sensitive knowledge. This is knowledge of nearby external objects in the present. This is inferential rather than direct, but he is troubled by the nature of the inference. It is not deduction, but it goes "beyond bare probability" and still "passes under the name of knowledge", even though it does not reach the certainty of intuition or demonstration. We have intuitive knowledge that "the idea we receive from an external object is in our minds", and from this infer the existence of the object (*Essay*: IV ii 14). For example, when I see a sheet of paper, I intuit that I have an idea of a white rectangular object and from this infer that there is a piece of paper here. The inference has the form:

  (1) I have an idea of a white rectangular object.
  Thus (2) There is a sheet of paper here.

The premise is known intuitively by reflecting on my sensation and the conclusion is sensitive knowledge, according to Locke. But the inference is not deductive, since I may have the idea when there is no paper before me; I may be dreaming or hallucinating. Furthermore, even if there is an object here, I may be misinterpreting the experience. It may not be a piece of paper, but the cover of a book. Locke is aware of this, but thinks that in favourable conditions "we are provided with an evidence, that puts us past doubting" (*ibid.*). When we look at the sun by day and think of it at night, he argues, we are conscious of the difference, so that our belief is not guessing or just a probable conjecture.

There are several problems with this. First, his official definition is that knowledge is certainty, yet the inference here is not deductive and, despite his claims, does not establish the conclusion with certainty. His reply is that its certainty is as great as we need for our happiness and pleasure, in other words, it is sufficient for practical purposes. But this misses the point. His claim that knowledge is certainty takes 'certainty' to be belief beyond any possible or imaginable doubt ("absolute certainty") and not belief sufficient for practical affairs ("moral certainty") or great assurance ("firm belief"). Such certainty does not admit of degrees; it either meets the standard or it does not. When Locke says that sensitive knowledge is knowledge because it is certain enough, he has clearly lowered the standard to include it. He seems to be aware of this, but glosses over the point. He says that anything short of intuition or demonstration "with what assurance soever embraced, is but faith or opinion", then adds "at least in all general truths" (*ibid.*). He explicitly lowers the standard so that what is faith in other matters qualifies as knowledge in the case of nearby external objects. Sensitive knowledge does not "reach perfectly" to the certainty of demonstration or intuition, but is still knowledge. Clearly, calling it knowledge is an honorary label. The more reasonable alternative would be to lower the standard of knowledge, but Locke hesitates to do this, probably because it would have been taken to be too great a concession to skepticism.

A second and more serious problem is the nature of the inference from (1) to (2). It is not deduction (in which the conclusion necessarily follows), but it does not seem to be a generalization from experience either (in technical language, an induction). We cannot tell by generalizing from experience that the idea is a reliable sign of an external object, since we are only directly aware of ideas. To claim that we know by experience that the idea is a sign of a real piece of paper assumes that we can correlate ideas with external objects and so assumes that we have knowledge of external objects. But this begs the question. We cannot justify an inference from one level of entities to another unless we have access to both levels; to assume we know something on the problematic level begs the question. This is one of the great issues for any empiricist theory of justification. We shall examine it when we consider skepticism in Chapter 6.

So far we have been dealing with Locke's empiricist theory of three of the major propositions about real existence: ourselves, God and external objects. Let us turn to his theory of science and his alternative to the Aristotelian-medieval and Cartesian theories of our knowledge of the ultimate nature of reality.

Nominal and real essences

We saw earlier that one of Descartes's motivations in defending innate ideas was to guarantee scientific knowledge by ensuring a correspondence between our basic categories and the world. Locke thinks there is a limited correspondence, but denies that we can have scientific knowledge in Descartes's sense. At best we have analogical conjectures. This was a skeptical conclusion in his day, but he downplayed it in the *Essay*. He says in the introduction that it would be "an unpardonable, as well as childish peevishness" to undervalue the knowledge we have and complain that some things are out of our reach. "The candle, that is set up in us, shines bright enough for all our purposes." If we can know all that is necessary to conduct our affairs and govern our opinions, we should not be troubled. "'Tis of great use to the sailor to know the length of his line, though he cannot with it fathom all the depths of the ocean" (*Essay*: I i 5, 6). Since his conception is similar to the modern view of science, we might conclude that Locke was a great prophet, but this distorts his role as a force in shaping the modern conception. He was as much a cause as a prophet.

Locke's view is based on his rejection of innate knowledge, his empiricism and his broadly Epicurean atomism. The properties we know by sensitive knowledge are only the outward appearances of things. The idea of gold, for example, is the idea of a fusible, malleable substance that is largely inert, dense and yellow; this is the *nominal essence* of gold. But we cannot know the "foundation from which all its properties flow" or the *real essence* (*Essay*: III iii 18; see also II xxxi 6ff.). The result is a two-tiered conception of the physical world (see key point "Levels of skepticism"). We perceive macro objects and create complex ideas of kinds, but we cannot know the configuration of the micro particles that explain the outward properties. Perception provides knowledge (just barely) at the sensible level, but it fails at the insensible and more explanatory level.

The conclusion Locke draws is that scientific knowledge of nature is impossible. The only evidence we can have about real essences is analogical, hypothetical and probable while scientific knowledge must be

Locke: Ideas are caused by physical objects and their qualities, which in turn are explained by insensible corpuscles (atoms).

Levels of reality	Propositions	Our knowledge
Ideas ↑	'I have an idea of red'	Known by intuition
Physical objects and their qualities ↑	'This is an apple'	Known by sensitive knowledge
Insensible particles	Laws about atoms	Believed with probability by analogy

Result: two skeptical problems:

1. How can we know physical objects if we cannot directly perceive them and knowledge must be certain?
2. How can we know the ultimate nature of matter?

Locke thinks we can have knowledge of physical objects, but not of insensible particles (since we do not have "microscopical eyes"). *Berkeley* later argued that nothing can be known beyond our ideas.

certain. His model for science here is Aristotelian (and Cartesian). This holds that a science is a deductive theory with self-evident axioms from which we can deduce laws that are certain. Geometry and arithmetic are sciences in this sense, but they are only about our ideas, whereas natural philosophy (physics and chemistry) is about real existence, but never gives more than probable conjectures. Locke sums up his view in this way:

> So that as to all general knowledge, we must search and find it only in our minds, and 'tis only by the examining of our own ideas, that furnisheth us with that. Truths belonging to essences of things, (that is, to abstract ideas) are eternal, and are to be found out only by the contemplation of those essences: as the existence of things is to be known only from experience.
>
> (*Essay*: IV iii 31)

Let us look at his theory of geometry then turn to natural philosophy. Locke holds that knowledge of the qualities of triangles is based on the abstract idea of triangularity, which does not have real existence but is created by abstraction. There is thus no distinction between the nominal essence and the real essence on which it is based. From the idea of triangle in general and other ideas we can deduce that the internal angles of a triangle equal two right angles and other theorems. But this does not imply that there are triangles in nature. To apply the theorems, we must know that there are real existences that satisfy the definition and the theorems, and this can only be known by experience. The result is *a priori* knowledge but not knowledge of real existence. Similar remarks apply to arithmetic, which is based on the abstract ideas of the numbers. The real and nominal essences are the same since both are present to the mind. (We shall have more to say about this is Chapter 5.)

In the case of natural philosophy, the real and nominal essences diverge. Complex ideas are combinations of simple (or simpler) ideas that derive from the powers of objects to cause them. The idea of gold is a complex idea also containing the idea of substance, which unites the qualities, since it is a substance idea as opposed to a mode idea; it is a "real" idea (since it represents an existing substance) as opposed to a "fantastical" idea like that of a mermaid. But it is not an adequate idea, since we have no reason to think it is complete (i.e. that it represents each of the individual powers of gold). It also differs from the *real essence* of gold, that is, the internal constitution of gold that explains its observable properties. Any ideas we have about this are analogical and so problematic as to be uninformative. In the case of mathematics, the nominal and real essences coincide and are accessible to us, but in the case of natural science only the nominal essence is accessible.

Locke makes two points about these essences in science. First, he argues that we have knowledge with certainty so long as we restrict our claims to nominal essences. We can know that gold is yellow and fusible because this is how we define 'gold'. Hence it is true by convention. But taken in this way, 'Gold is yellow and fusible' does not imply real existence. The result is a kind of natural science based on classification, but a science that does not by itself tell us about reality. To apply it, we have to know that there is a substance matching the definition and this can only be known empirically. The result is a dilemma: if the proposition refers to the abstract idea of gold alone, it is true by definition but uninformative, while, if it refers to the substance, it can be justified only by generalization from sense experience and not known with certainty (although it will then be informative). In neither case can we have genuine science of reality in the traditional sense.

Secondly, Locke thinks knowledge of physical real essences is logically possible, since God could have given us the means to know them empirically. If we had "microscopical eyes" (eyes that could see configured atoms, not very tiny eyes), we could perceive real essences and perhaps deduce the macro qualities of physical objects. The result would be a genuine physical science in which natural laws are deduced from more fundamental laws in a way comparable to the way theorems about triangles are deduced from the abstract idea of triangularity. The laws governing the insensible particles and their relation to the macro qualities would be known with certainty just as Aristotle and Descartes hoped. Locke even suggests that with such eyes we could know that these laws are necessary truths similar to those in mathematics. But these are all hopes, according to Locke, since we do not have microscopical eyes.

This throws light on Locke's conception of (justificatory) empiricism. First, he holds that the principle of empiricism (namely, that all knowledge of real existence rests on experience) is not itself a necessary truth but is true because we do not have such eyes. His view seems to be that if, contrary to fact, we could perceive real essences of physical objects, we would have fully adequate ideas of their constitutions. It might be thought that the result would be an *empirical* science of atomic structure, but this is not what he means. Microscopical eyes would give us particular ideas of the ultimate particles from which we could frame abstract ideas. Then, by examining these, we would come to know the axioms and from these deduce the macro qualities. The result would be *a priori* knowledge of laws of nature parallel to our knowledge of mathematics, just as Descartes hoped. But this is only a dream, since we do not have such powers. (Indeed he argues that God was wise not to give us microscopical eyes, since they would be detrimental to practice. How could we eat an apple or find the door, if we perceived all the atoms between us and the apple and door? And how alluring would prospective mates be if we could see all their inner workings?)

The second point is that Locke does not think that (justificatory) empiricism is inconsistent with the laws of nature being necessary truths. Most accounts of empiricism hold that laws cannot be neces-

---

Locke's style

Earthly minds, like mud walls, resist the strongest batteries: and though, perhaps, sometimes the force of a clear argument may make some impression, yet they nevertheless stand firm, keep out the enemy truth, that would captivate, or disturb them. Tell a man, passionately in love, that he is jilted; bring a score of witnesses of the falsehood of his mistress, 'tis ten to one but three kind words of hers, shall invalidate all their testimonies.

(*Essay*: IV xx 12)

sary unless they are *a priori*. But Locke thinks we might have probable empirical evidence that a universal proposition *L* is true even though *L* is a necessary truth. When we frame conjectures about real essences, we might hit on a law statement that is true and necessarily so, even though our evidence is empirical. Most subsequent empiricists have held that if *L* is a necessary truth, we must be able to learn that it is true by reflecting on its constituent ideas (and other propositions), that is, we must be able to learn it *a priori*. But Locke makes a sharper distinction between the way in which we come to know that something is true and the kind of fact it is; that is, he makes a sharper distinction between the epistemic status of a proposition and the ontological status of the fact it purports to depict.

Summary

In this chapter, we have discussed:

- Locke's and Descartes's reactions to the Aristotelian-medieval theory of science and perception;
- Descartes's rejection of abstraction in favour of innate ideas and Locke's more skeptical alternative;
- Locke's rejection of innate speculative knowledge and innate ideas, as well as Leibniz's objections;
- Locke's theory of ideas and how they derive from experience;
- Locke's theory of the three degrees of knowledge – intuitive, demonstrative and sensitive – and his doubts about the possibility of an adequate science of real essences.

two

Berkeley's defence of idealism

Berkeley agrees with Locke that physical objects and God can only be known by experience, that the self is known by reflection, and that mathematics does not give us knowledge of real existence; he is thus an empiricist. But he rejects Locke's claim that physical objects are distinct from ideas and composed of insensible material particles. He takes this to be unempirical and meaningless on empirical grounds (since they are insensible) and even contradictory (since we cannot think of something completely independent of thought).

As we saw, Locke holds that the mind directly perceives ideas and indirectly perceives real physical objects. Since the idea is distinct from the material object and the idea's existence in the mind does not imply that the object exists, Berkeley holds that the empirical is restricted to our ideas and that matter is unknowable. A strict empiricism is inconsistent with the existence of matter and the only way to defend it, according to Berkeley, is to make the distinction between appearance and reality within the realm of ideas and not between ideas and non-ideas. Berkeley calls this doctrine immaterialism, but its more usual name is *idealism*; Locke's theory is a version of *realism*. Let us look more closely at these theories.

In general, to be a realist about a range of entities is to claim that they are real and exist independently of what is thought about them. One may be a realist about universals such as redness and goodness (as Plato was) or a realist about moral facts (a moral realist). The form of realism Berkeley attacks is realism about physical objects. In Locke's version, physical objects are independent of what is thought about them since

> **KEY POINT** *Realism and idealism*
>
> To be a *realist* about a domain *X* is to hold that entities in *X* are real, that is, exist independently of what is thought about them.
> - *Physical realism*: physical objects exist independently of thought.
> - *Idealism* (Berkeley's immaterialism): physical objects do not exist independently of thought, but must be perceived by some mind, that is "To be is to be perceived" (*Esse est percipi*).

they are material and matter contrasts with the mental. If we define a *material object* as a non-mental physical object independent of what anyone thinks about it, we can say that this form of realism, which we may call *physical realism*, holds that there are material objects, while *idealism* holds that there are no material objects. These theses contradict each other, but one might withhold judgement about them and claim skepticism. Idealism and realism are metaphysical doctrines, but skepticism is an epistemological position, since it neither asserts nor denies the existence of material objects, but only denies knowledge of them. Berkeley argues that Locke's realism leads to skepticism, which he rejects on common-sense grounds. He also thinks realism encourages skepticism about religious belief. Idealism, he argues, can put an end to both forms of skepticism and lead to a more acceptable form of empiricism.

At first glance, this appears absurd and even more at odds with common sense than Locke's claim that we do not directly perceive physical objects. How can we recognize the reality of the physical world if we reduce it to ideas? And how can idealism be the only alternative to skepticism? Surely it would be more plausible to turn to rationalism. Berkeley himself was much ridiculed by his contemporaries. A wit once wrote to Jonathan Swift, for example, that poor George had *the idea of a fever* and could not get over it.

In this chapter we shall consider Berkeley's answer to these questions, his positive arguments for idealism and his criticism of Locke. Aside from its intrinsic interest, his philosophy raises what is perhaps the central question for empiricism: whether it can explain our preanalytic convictions about knowledge of the external world without lapsing into idealism or skepticism.

Berkeley's arguments

Berkeley has three main arguments to support his idealism: an argument from common sense; an *a priori* argument, which he takes to be the central one; and an argument based on the impossibility of matter causing ideas.

The common-sense argument

This holds that we directly perceive physical objects and that the only objects of direct perception are ideas. Thus, since ideas are dependent on mind, it must follow that physical objects are also dependent on mind or, as he puts it, that to be is to be perceived (*PHK*: §1–3). We may set this out as follows:

> (1) Physical objects are directly perceived.
> (2) Only ideas are directly perceived.
> (3) Ideas are dependent on what is thought about them.
> Thus (4) Physical objects are dependent on thought.

The premise that we directly perceive the physical world (i.e. (1)) is something we all believe, according to Berkeley. When we see an apple, we naturally believe that it and its qualities (its shape, colour and feel) are directly present to us. We do not think that we are aware of ideas or images in the mind from which we infer its existence; no such inference occurs. He takes the second premise (that we directly perceive only ideas) to be self-evident. Premise (3) (that ideas are dependent on what is thought about them) he takes to be true by definition.

The argument rests on common sense because the first premise is a thesis of common sense, according to Berkeley. But there is a problem with this. Common sense also holds that physical objects exist when no one is thinking about them. The logs in the fire continue to burn when the room is empty, but if they are ideas, as Berkeley claims, there must still be *some mind* perceiving them and common sense does not accept this.

The result is that the appeal to common sense is inconclusive. The ordinary person believes both that we directly perceive physical objects *and* that they exist independently of whether anyone is perceiving them. If the rest of Berkeley's argument is correct, common sense is contradictory and cannot be used selectively as Berkeley does. Common sense is committed to both direct perception and the denial of Berkeley's conclusion.

The a priori *argument*

Berkeley rests his entire case on the second argument. He says that if you can conceive of an "extended movable substance" to exist "otherwise than in a mind perceiving it", he will "give up the cause." He thinks this is impossible since if you think of books or trees existing unperceived, "do you not yourself perceive or think of them all the time?" In order to show that there is something independent of mind, you must conceive of it existing unconceived, and so conceive of it all the while. When we try to conceive of physical objects existing unperceived, the mind takes "no notice of itself" and is deluded into thinking that unperceived things are conceivable. That there are unperceived physical objects, as Locke claims, is thus "a manifest repugnancy" or contradiction: "the absolute existence of unthinking things are words without a meaning, or which include a contradiction" (*PHK*: §§22–4).

This argument makes a stronger claim than the first. The first rests on common sense, which may be mistaken, whereas the second claims that the realist's thesis is a contradiction. If correct, this would mean that Berkeley's thesis 'To be is to be conceived' (or *Esse est percipi*) is a necessary truth similar to 'To be a triangle is to have three sides'. Idealism then does not rest on a dubious assumption of common sense, but can be proved *a priori*.

Berkeley's argument is a reduction to absurdity: the realist hypothesis implies a contradiction and so is false. The realist holds (1), which implies (2), which in turn implies (3), which is a contradiction. Hence, 1 must be false.

> (1) *S* is thinking that there is something he is not
>   thinking about.   (Assumption)
> Thus (2) There is something that *S* is thinking about and not
>   thinking about at the same time.
> Thus (3) There is something that is *F* and *not-F* at the same
>   time.

Unfortunately the argument is not valid. It professes to show that it is a necessary truth that to exist is to be perceived, where perceiving is taken to be the most general mental operation one can perform on an object of thought, and includes more specific mental operations such as believing, conceiving, perceiving (in the usual sense of external perception), wondering and thinking about. This is equivalent to holding that it is impossible for something to exist and not be perceived, that is, that '*x* exists without being perceived' is a contradiction. The argument for this is that I cannot think of *x* existing without "perceiving" *x*, that is, without thinking of it. But this only proves that 'I am thinking of *x* existing without thinking of *x*' is a contradiction. It does not show that

'x exists and no one is thinking of x' is a contradiction. 'I am thinking of x existing' or alternatively 'I am thinking that x exists' is not the same thought as 'x exists'. All Berkeley's argument shows is that I cannot think of something without thinking of it. To think of something without thinking of it is a contradiction, but it does not show that someone must be perceiving the object for it to exist.

The contradiction Berkeley is appealing to is sometimes called a pragmatic contradiction, since the circumstances under which the proposition is considered contradict what it claims. For example, if I say that I cannot speak, I contradict myself, since in saying anything at all, I show that I can speak. If I *write* that I cannot speak, there is no contradiction, but I cannot both be dumb and *say* that I am. Similarly, if I say that I do not exist, my *saying* this shows that I exist, since in order to say anything at all, I must exist. The contradiction here is: x says that x does not exist, and x does not exist. The first conjunct contradicts the second. But this does not show that the proposition that x does not exist is a contradiction. The contradiction is a substitution instance of 'x says that p, and x does not exist' where p is any proposition.

Consider the following entailments:

(1) x exists → x is perceived.
(2) S thinks that x exists → x is perceived.

The first is equivalent to Berkeley's thesis *Esse est percipi*, where x ranges over physical objects. Berkeley must show that this is true in order to prove that nothing can exist unperceived, but all he shows is that (2) is true. And this only shows that S cannot think of something existing without perceiving it.

The explanatory argument

The third argument is not explained in detail, but is alluded to in several places. Berkeley argues that we are certain that we are spirits and have ideas, but it is beyond the power of brute matter to explain either spirits or ideas. We might think it is easy "to conceive and explain the manner of their production" from matter, but even the materialists, that is, realists, admit that they cannot "comprehend in what manner body can act upon spirit, or how it is possible it should imprint any idea in the mind". Hence matter is useless as a hypothesis. The production of ideas is "equally inexplicable with, or without this supposition" (*PHK*: §19). Berkeley also argues that matter is by definition inactive. In common speech, it signifies "extended, solid, movable, unthinking, inactive substance". And, even if we admit it exists, how can "that which is *inactive* be a *cause*; or that which is *unthinking* be a *cause of thought*?" We may change the meaning and hold that matter is active, but this is just "to play with words" (*Dialogue* II: 164–5).

Viewed in this light, idealism is an alternative explanation to realism. Locke held that ideas of colours are caused by powers in external objects, which in turn rest on their material constitution. If Berkeley is right, this is not an adequate explanation. The material cannot cause the immaterial, so matter plays no explanatory role and is unnecessary. This poses a dilemma for the realist. If he holds that minds and ideas exist in addition to matter and that ideas are caused by material changes in physical things, he has to explain how there can be such a causal relation. If, on the other hand, he denies the existence of minds and ideas, and holds that only matter exists (as materialism in the strict sense does), he must deny our obvious and self-evident knowledge that it does. Since neither option is acceptable, idealism is the only acceptable alternative. Only minds and ideas exist, and belief in an independent material world is an illusion.

Looked at in this way, Berkeley's idealism is a broadly empirical theory in competition with realism and materialism, that is, the theory that only matter exists. But the issue is more complicated than this. There is also a fourth theory. Leibniz held that physical objects exist independently of what we think of them since they are composed of monads or "little" minds that exist independently of each other. This is also a version of immaterialism, but it is distinct from Berkeley's. It is a form of atomism in which the "atoms" composing the world are mental substances rather than material atoms. Leibniz holds that physical objects exist when no one perceives them, since they are composed of mind atoms similar to the naturalist's atoms except that they are immaterial, whereas Berkeley holds that physical objects require a mind perceiving them. Leibniz, in short, is a realist without matter, a view often referred to as *panpsychism*. There are also other theories, so Berkeley's argument does not refute realism by itself.

Berkeley does not claim that this is as decisive as the *a priori* argument. It also rests on an assumption Locke would not accept. Locke thinks it is possible for matter to think and hence possible for material objects to cause changes that result in ideas in the mind. He does not accept Berkeley's claim that matter is useless as an explanatory principle. To the claim that we cannot show how matter can affect thought, a Lockean might reply that we have to wait on further developments of science and not rush to the conclusion that it is impossible. As Epicurus once said when asked whether a tower in the distance was round or square, wait: if we cannot tell now, we should put off the question until we get closer.

Some misconceptions

Let us turn to some of the details of Berkeley's theory and its relation to empiricism. I want to consider three questions: in what sense can immaterialism recognize the existence of "real things" as he calls them; is his idealism consistent with empiricism; and can he can defend idealism without appeal to God?

Does Berkeley deny "real things"?

Berkeley is adamant that his theory does not reduce the world to illusion. Real things are not material substances but ideas forced on us in coherent sequences. Two marks distinguish them from ideas of imagination and illusions. They are (i) independent of our will and (ii) have "a steadiness, order, and coherence" and do not appear at random like ideas of imagination and illusions (*PHK*: §29–30). If I think about my car in the driveway, the idea before my mind is less vivid than when I look out of the window and see it. Ideas of sense also cohere in a way memory images do not. If the object I sense is real, I can look again or go outside and perceive it from different angles. The remembered idea is more or less a single image and can be changed by an act of will, but "real thing" ideas cannot be. In both cases, according to Berkeley, I am aware of nothing but ideas, but I take one set to be the real thing and the other an idea of the imagination.

In support of this, he says that when we say something is real, we mean nothing more than that it is a set of coherent ideas forced on us. When the door is closed and I try to leave the room, I have ideas of the door, its colour and shape, and ideas of the door knob. If I try to walk through it, I find that I have further sensations, a bump on the head and a closer view of its surface. These ideas cannot be willed away, no matter how hard I try. To get into the other room, I have to turn the knob and open the door; that is, I have to perform certain actions that result in further ideas being forced on me. The actions are under my control, but the resulting ideas are not. As a result, I conclude rightly that the door is real and is closed but, according to Berkeley, it is nothing but a set of ideas.

Berkeley thinks some imagined events are forced on us, but fail the second test. If I dream that I am driving a red sports car, the ideas seem to be real things, so real that I believe I am actually doing it. Nightmares deceive us in this way. But when we wake up, we have ideas of the ceiling and the bedcovers that do not cohere with the dream ideas. In such cases, the ideas fail the coherence test and are judged to be unreal.

Berkeley's criteria draw the distinction between reality and appearance within the broader class of ideas. It is interesting to note that the realist also accepts them as tests of reality. The difference is that he takes them to be criteria for determining when an idea refers to a material object independent of all thought and when it does not, that is, as marks that help us to discover when we are perceiving an independent object, while Berkeley takes them to be the defining characteristics of real things. Reality, on his account, is the orderly progression of ideas we are forced to accept and has no basis in matter.

One consequence of this is that Berkeley alters the meaning of real existence found in Locke and others. Locke holds that x has real existence if and only if x is independent of what *anyone* thinks about it, while Berkeley holds that the real is independent of what you or I or any finite number of minds think about it, but not of *every* mind, since his idealism commits him to holding that to be is to be perceived by *some* mind. There is no existence outside the realm of spirits and their mental contents. Physical objects do not have absolute independence from thought, but only independence from the localized thought of you and me, and human beings in general. As a result, his empiricism is only committed to the view that all knowledge of real existence in this relativized sense depends on experience. We might argue that this does not make him an empiricist in Locke's sense, but I think this is hasty. Empiricism is an epistemological doctrine while real existence is a metaphysical notion. To be an empiricist is to hold that experience is the only source of justification of claims of real existence, and leaves the explicit definition of 'real existence' to metaphysics. The dispute between Locke and Berkeley is over the nature of reality, not over the source of our knowledge of it.

Is Berkeley an empiricist?

A second question is whether Berkeley's principle "*Esse est percipi*" is consistent with empiricism. It may seem it is not, since it is both *a priori* and about existence, but it is. The empiricist holds that knowledge that something has real existence must be empirical, but this does not imply that knowledge that something does *not* exist must be empirical. Knowledge of non-existence can be empirical or *a priori*. I know empirically that there are no elephants in the room, but my knowledge that there are no round squares is *a priori*. Being round and square at the same time are incompatible qualities, so we know *a priori* that there cannot be such things. According to Berkeley, material objects are in the same category as round squares. For there to be a material object, we would have to conceive of it and not conceive of it simultaneously, and, as we saw, Berkeley thinks this is impossible. He may be mistaken in thinking that idealism can be proved *a priori*, but his believing this is consistent with empiricism.

He does not discuss and defend empiricism specifically, but assumes it as the general framework. In this he is a good Lockean, despite his other disagreements with Locke. He holds that we know by reflection that our ideas exist and that we are immaterial substances. Furthermore, real things are known by sense experience. We know that the earth is real because we can walk on it and it is hard to our touch, and that the sun exists because we can see it and feel its warmth – that is, by sensation. He also holds that numbers and geometrical objects are fictions and hence that our *a priori* knowledge of mathematics is not about real things, but about ideas of the imagination, just as Locke did. He also rejects conceptual arguments for God's existence. He calls such arguments "metaphysical" and has a character in a later dialogue say that such arguments "I have always found dry and jejune; and, as they are not suited to my way of thinking, they may perhaps puzzle me, but never will convince me" (*Alciphron* IV: §2, 85). The only arguments for God's existence he accepts rest on the existence, order and coherence of nature and are empirical. Sometimes he alludes to the argument from design (i.e. that we know that God exists because of the order we find in nature), but his main argument rests on his idealism, which we must now consider.

Does idealism require God?

As we noted, Berkeley holds that something can be real only if a mind is perceiving it. The question is: who is perceiving ideas that make up things we consider to be real, but which no one has ever perceived? Before spacecraft orbited the moon, no one had ever seen the side that is always turned away from earth, yet we believe that there was another side all the same, with rocks, craters and ridges existing for eons unperceived by any human being or animal. Nor has anyone perceived what is hundreds of miles below the earth's surface. Berkeley's answer is that God is perceiving all of these things even though no one else is. Given the truth of idealism and that the rocks and craters on the moon are real, some spirit must have the ideas that compose them and this spirit is God, according to Berkeley.

This leads to an alternative characterization of real things. Physical things are ideas impressed on us by an infinite being with the power to force them on us and the omniscience to perceive all of them at once. This suggests that Berkeley holds that God takes the place of matter in a realist metaphysics. Instead of having senseless matter guarantee the fixity and reality of the real things, he reduces things to ideas and appeals to an infinite mind to maintain their order and coherence. This has led to much ridicule and satire (see "A limerick").

This reliance on God has several consequences for Berkeley's immaterialism. First, as we suggested, it appears to undermine his attempt to support idealism by appealing to common sense. It may be common sense that we directly perceive physical objects, but few would agree that they are just ideas made stable because God is always thinking them. Secondly, it might be argued that it is impious to think that he could not have material objects do the work for him. Berkeley's position is not contradictory, but it is not common sense either, as his first argument claims.

It is not clear that this is a fair representation of Berkeley's position. He believes that God exists and perceives everything all the time, but he does not simply *assume* his existence as the limerick suggests in order to make his metaphysics work. He holds that idealism is defensible without appeal to God and offers an argument for his existence. In fact, his main argument for God appeals to idealism as a premise. Let us look at this.

A limerick

There once was a man who said, "God
Must find it exceedingly odd
    If he finds that this tree
    Continues to be
When there's no one about in the Quad."   (Ronald Knox)

Dear Sir, Your astonishment's odd;
I am always about in the Quad.
    And that's why the tree
    Will continue to be,
Since observed by yours faithfully, God.   (Anonymous reply)

He holds (1) that to be is to be perceived, or, as we have put it, that physical things are coherent bundles of ideas, on the basis of the three arguments considered in the previous section and (2) that we know that there are real things on empirical grounds, since we cannot will them away and our ideas form orderly patterns. He concludes (3) "There is therefore some other will or spirit that produces them" (*PHK*: §29). Furthermore, since experience teaches us that this power exceeds that of all human beings combined, this will must be great enough to hold all the details of nature in its mind and so must be infinite, as God is taken to be. Summarized, the argument is:

(1) Idealism is true: for physical objects, to be is to be perceived.
(2) There are physical objects.
Thus (3) There is an infinitely powerful spirit, that is, God.

If we accept Berkeley's claim that immaterialism rests entirely on the *a priori* argument, the first premise is known *a priori*. The second is based on experience. Hence the argument as a whole is empirical, since any argument with an empirical premise is empirical. Furthermore, if this interpretation is correct, his idealism does not assume God's existence.

Two points should be noted about Berkeley's argument. First, like most arguments for God, there is a gap between what the premises warrant and what the conclusion asserts. Our experience shows only that there is a spirit with the power to force ideas on all humanity combined and capable of creating ideas that make up our finite physical world, but it does not follow that it is *infinite* in either power or knowledge. We can only conclude that he has enough power to create the effect, and since this is finite, it does not follow that he is infinite. Secondly, as we saw, Berkeley cannot appeal to God to defend idealism, since this would bring in the conclusion (3) to defend premise (1), and make the argument circular. God may always be about in the quad, but Berkeley cannot appeal to him to show that the trees in the quad exist when we are not around. He must be able to show that they have continued existence on independent grounds. This is characteristic of all explanatory arguments. The facts to be explained must be established without appeal to the unproved features of the explanation.

The first point is not a criticism of Berkeley in particular, since all empirical arguments for God suffer from the same defect. At most these arguments prove a supreme being, not an infinitely powerful one. But this would still be a significant accomplishment, if he can defend ideal-ism independently. The second is more serious. Berkeley must be able to answer objections to immaterialism on conceptual or empirical grounds without appealing to God. To bring in God might make immaterialism a coherent overall account of the world, but it would not live up to Berkeley's intentions for it. It would not silence the skeptic nor resolve our religious doubts, since no skeptic or non-believer would consent to a reply to an objection that appealed to God as an assumption. It is not clear that Berkeley's theory can satisfy this requirement, despite his intentions. He often replies to objections by bringing in God. This may be because he thinks that the *a priori* argument is so conclusive that no objection has any weight against it. The appeal to God then is only a way to silence the critic until he comes to see the truth of idealism; working out the details is not worth pursuing. Unfortunately, this puts a weight on the master argument that it cannot bear. As we saw, there are strong reasons to think it is invalid and the common-sense argument is also not conclusive. This means that the third argument, namely, the explanatory argument, must stand on its own and be defensible without appeals to God. This raises interesting questions about Berkeley's philosophy, but we cannot pursue them here.

The attack on Locke

Berkeley attacks Locke on several grounds. Here we shall consider his criticisms of: his account of abstract ideas; the idea of substance; and the distinction between primary and secondary qualities. A fourth criti-cism, namely, that material objects are unknowable on Locke's theory, will be discussed in Chapter 6.

Abstract ideas

As we have seen, abstraction plays an important part in Locke's rejection of Descartes's theory of innate ideas. Ideas that Descartes takes to be innate are abstracted from experience, according to Locke. Although he does not agree with Descartes, Berkeley does not agree with Locke either. He holds that we can abstract ideas of qualities or parts of objects only if it is possible for them to exist apart from them. If *B* cannot exist separately from *A*, we cannot abstract *B* from *A*. We can abstract the idea of a human being's arm from the idea of his body, since an arm can exist without a body, but we cannot abstract the redness of a cherry from its shape. We might imagine it as having some other colour, but we cannot think of the colour without also having an idea of shape. If Berkeley is right about this, our ideas and what we can intelligibly think about are severely restricted in three ways:

- We cannot distinguish existence from perception and claim, as the realist does, that there are objects independent of perception.
- We cannot distinguish ideas of secondary qualities (such as colour) from those of primary qualities, which in turn implies that we cannot conceive of insensible particles that are colourless and odourless, but are still solid, extended and in motion; that is, the new science cannot be interpreted as showing us that there is a world of matter behind sensible appearance.
- The notions of material substance and qualities as powers are also meaningless, since we have no ideas of them but only of their effects on us.

Let us look at Berkeley's criticism of abstraction more closely.

Berkeley has two arguments. The first is that, since we cannot frame an idea of what is contradictory, if it is impossible for X and Y to exist separately, we cannot frame an idea of X without Y. Since a limb and the body of an animal can exist apart, we can abstract the idea of the limb from that of the body, but we cannot abstract redness from extension, since it is impossible for something red not to be extended. He says that he can frame the idea of a man with two heads or of "the upper parts of a man joined to the body of a horse", but he cannot frame an idea of a body without a particular shape and figure and make an abstract idea that contains distinguishing properties of the being without any particular ones. We cannot frame an abstract notion "by abstracting from particulars" and not considering other consequent qualities (*PHK: Intro.* §10).

A second argument is that Locke's account implies that abstract ideas have contradictory qualities (*PHK: Intro.* §13). He quotes Locke's remark that it requires "some pains and skill to form the *general* idea of a *triangle*" since it must be "neither oblique, nor rectangle, neither equilateral, equicrural, nor scalenon, but all and none of these at once" (*Essay*: IV vii 9). An abstract idea not only lacks the qualities that make it a specific three-sided figure, but it has the qualities of all the specific kinds even though they contradict one another. Clearly, Berkeley says, no one can form "the abstract idea of a triangle" that is neither oblique nor rectangular but both of these at once.

Neither of these objections shows that there are no abstract ideas in Locke's sense. Locke holds that we abstract the idea of whiteness by noting the similarity between particular ideas, such as snow, milk and chalk, and not attending to their dissimilarities. The abstract idea is the idea of this similarity. We arrive at it by disregarding what is peculiar to each particular idea and considering only the similarity. The concepts of substance and powers distinct from appearances are also abstract ideas. We form them by thinking of the similarity between particular substances of the same or different species (two human beings or a human being and a horse). They are not abstract pictures or images of the similarities with no details, but thoughts of similarities that we make general by "considering them as they are in the mind such appearances, separate from all other existences" (*Essay*: II xi 9). In another place he calls this "partial consideration" and distinguishes it from separation:

> A man may consider light in the Sun, without its heat; or mobility [velocity] in body without its extension, without thinking of their separation. One is only a partial consideration, terminating in one alone; and the other is a consideration of both, as existing separately. (*Essay*: II xiii 13)

Locke's point is that to abstract is to consider or think of one thing or quality *as* separate from another; it is not to think *that* it is separate. When we abstract the light of the sun from its heat, we consider the light without considering its heat, but we do not consider that it has light without heat. Similarly when I abstract whiteness from chalk and snow, I think of the chalk's similarity to snow without thinking of its cylindrical shape, but I do not think that the chalk is only white and not cylindrical or shapeless.

This distinction between considering one quality separately from another and thinking it to be separate is found in medieval discussions of abstraction and would have been a commonplace in Locke's day. To abstract a quality that is inseparable from another is not to contradict oneself, unless you also judge that the abstracted quality can exist separately, and this is not to abstract, but to believe falsely that it can exist without the other quality. Berkeley is thus mistaken in thinking that to abstract is to separate.

This gives us another perspective on the principle "*Esse est percipi*". Berkeley claims that we cannot abstract existence from perception or conception, since every time we think of something as existing, we conceive of it. This is true, but it does not follow that we cannot think of it as existing without thinking of it as being conceived. The realist holds that it is no more difficult to think of an object existing unperceived than to think of the whiteness of snow without thinking of its coldness. In fact, this is how we use existential quantifiers. When a man is found shot to death, we know that he was killed by *someone*, without knowing specifically who it was. We can also know that a dead deer by the side of the road was struck by *some* vehicle or other without knowing its colour, size or make. In the same way, we can express our belief that something exists unconceived without knowing further details about it.

Berkeley's error is to take ideas to be images, that is, picture-like representations, the mental equivalent of photographic images recorded on film. Since we cannot have an image of an apple's colour that does not include its shape and size, Berkeley is right if Locke takes ideas to be images. But this is not Locke's view. He holds that to have an idea of *X* is to be able to think of *X* whether we have an image of it before our minds or not. He also equates ideas with the meanings of words, so that 'idea' is a general term including images and concepts. On his use of the term, to understand the meaning of a word or to have something "before the mind", is to have an idea of it. It might be argued that 'idea' in Locke's day had the narrower meaning of being an image, but this is no defence of Berkeley. An objection must take account of what the author says he means by his technical terminology and criticize it on these grounds, not on the grounds of what we ordinarily mean by it.

Two further points are of interest about this issue. First, Berkeley admits that we can think of God and other minds without having images of them. In the first edition of *Principles of Human Knowledge*, he restricted ideas to images and did not explain how we can think about ourselves and other spirits, but in later editions he introduced what he called notions. We have *ideas* of physical things, but *notions* of active beings such as ourselves, other people and God. We have a notion, he says, when "we understand the meaning of a word, otherwise we could not affirm or deny anything of it" (*PHK*: §140). Although Berkeley does not admit it, this is a concession to the Lockean account of ideas.

Berkeley assumes that a representation (whether an idea or a notion) must resemble its object. He holds that ideas cannot resemble material objects because they are radically different kinds of entities. We also cannot have an idea of an active spirit, since ideas are inert and not active. But this is a mistake. Representations do not have to be resemblances. The word 'man' represents human beings even though it does not resemble them. Representation is not a natural relation, but an intentional one we impose on signs.

Secondly, Berkeley agrees with Locke about how signs become general. He holds that we think about triangles in general by means of a particular triangle whose individuating features we ignore, and this is just what Locke holds. Neither thinks there is an abstract idea that is not scalene, right or equilateral. All ideas are particular in their existence and become general by how we use them. The difference is that Locke thinks it is harmless (and useful) to think of them as substantives (as we think of fictional characters as if they are real for some purposes), while Berkeley thinks such talk is illicit.

This throws light on Locke's example of the triangle. His point is that framing abstract ideas is difficult, since it is hard for most people to consider abstract similarities between things. 'Triangle' stands for everything that is an enclosed three-sided figure and represents right, equilateral, scalene and obtuse triangles even though none of these characteristics are part of its definition. It thus applies to "all and none" of them at once. When Berkeley quotes the passage in which Locke makes this point, he italicizes "all and none" where there are no italics in the original, emphasizing for his own purposes something that Locke passes over as a rhetorical flourish of no consequence (see *PHK: Intro.* §13).

The idea of substance

On the surface, Berkeley's criticism of Locke on substance seems straightforward, but there is also reason to think it is misplaced. He complains that Locke has no clear conception of substance, but has to rely on metaphors that it "upholds" or "supports" qualities. Berkeley is right to be suspicious of such talk, but Locke makes the same criticism. He thinks the concept of substance is supposed to explain the unity of qualities in objects, but fails to do so because of its obscurity (*Essay:* II xiii 19). Berkeley's real objection is to the idea of *material* substance, that is, to matter and its role as a support of qualities. But this is a criticism of matter as an explanatory principle, not of substance itself.

Berkeley says that extension is supposed to be an accident of matter and "that matter is the *substratum* that supports it" (*PHK:* §§16–17). But, he says, he has no idea of matter or its supporting qualities. 'Support' cannot be taken literally as when we say that pillars support a building, so the materialist must explain in what sense it supports. Later he says the original theory as held by the Greeks was that *all* qualities exist in a substratum and that this explains how they can exist independent of mind. Then the qualities of colour, sound and smell were eliminated from this, leaving only extension, solidity, motion and shape. But he thinks there is no longer any reason to posit any material substratum and, given his arguments for idealism, "it is utterly impossible that there should be such a thing". He thinks that men have given up the thing and retained the name to apply to "I know not what abstracted and indefinite notions of *being*, or *occasion*" (*PHK*: §§73–4).

One weakness in this is that Berkeley also claims that human beings and God are substances, albeit spiritual substances. If substance is an empty concept, how can he claim there are any? His answer is that we have immediate knowledge of ourselves as thinking beings, so 'thinking substance' is not a meaningless term: the substratum is not an unknown support in this case, since it is known. "That ideas should exist in what does not perceive, or be produced by what does not act, is repugnant. But it is no repugnancy to say, that a perceiving thing should be the subject of ideas, or an active thing the cause of them" (*Dialogue* III: 180).

It is not clear that this solves the problem. We may be directly aware that we are substances, but this does not make the concept less problematic. Furthermore, his objection to *material* substance is not to the conception of substance, but to the claim that matter can explain ideas. It is also not clear that we directly perceive the self as a substance. Hume later argued that, when he attempts to perceive the self directly, an idea (in the broad sense that includes Berkeley's notions) always intervenes. He is directly aware of the idea but not of the self as its subject. The result is that, even in the case of spiritual substances, the substance is a posit and Berkeley cannot rightly claim to understand the notion of spiritual substance by direct awareness.

In other places, Berkeley offers an alternative account that is consistent with Hume's view. He argues that the concept of substance is a relative idea and that we know spiritual substance only as the unknown support of perception and willing. Curiously enough, this is just what Locke says about the idea of substance in the *Essay*. All we have is an obscure relative idea of what the substance does (i.e. support qualities) without any explanation of how it does this (*Essay*: II xxiii 3).

The concept of a relative idea is medieval. We have a relative idea of an object when our only knowledge of it is that it bears some relation to something we can experience. For instance, if we find a wing in the forest, we have a relative idea of the bird it came from. We also have a relative idea of God as the creator of the universe without knowing him as he is in himself. Locke's point is that all we know about substratum is that it makes something a substance, but we do not know what it is in itself. It is an unknown something that unifies the perceived qualities into a single thing. It is often thought that he takes this to be explanatory and that this is the point of Berkeley's ridicule, but he does not. If anything he has even more disdain for it as an explanation.

There are two differences between him and Berkeley. First, he thinks that the concept was introduced to solve a genuine problem, namely, what makes some sets of perceived qualities unified objects rather than fictions. It is not clear that Berkeley thinks this is a problem at all. Some ideas make discrete objects and some do not, and that is the end of the matter. What unifies them ultimately is that God impresses them on us in a unified and orderly manner. Secondly, Locke holds that a relative idea can be meaningful even if we have never experienced the relatum. That is, we can meaningfully extend the relation beyond experienced conjunctions of the related objects and posit an analogous relation between something we perceive and something we never perceive and that is perhaps unperceivable. In the medieval example, we have perceived both of the related items in the past, namely, the wings and the birds, but in the case of God we have only experienced the world. Berkeley does not accept this. He thinks we have a relative idea only when we have perceived similar objects conjoined in the past. Since we do not have this in the case of matter supporting qualities, there cannot be a meaningful relative idea here. (Berkeley also denies that we have only a relative idea of God as the creator (*PHK*: §16).)

Primary and secondary qualities

Berkeley's attack on this distinction is an extension of his general criticism of matter and material substance. Locke holds that substances in the ordinary sense, for example, grains of sand, tables, trees, animals up to planets, are collections of insensible particles. Their unity and macro qualities are united by physical forces, but we have no explanation of what holds each particle together or what explains its qualities. Each particle is a substance with the qualities of extension, shape, motion, unity and solidity. These are the *primary qualities* in the sense that they are the qualities of the basic entities. The colour, sound, smell and taste of the object are *secondary qualities*, since only composites of particles have them. Their configurations cause us to have ideas of colour, sound, taste and smell, but nothing in the object resembles these ideas. Material substratum enters Locke's theory at the micro level, as the unknown principle that supposedly explains the corpuscle's primary qualities.

Berkeley's criticism of material substance is one prong of his attack on this theory. The other is his attack on the distinction between primary and secondary qualities. He has two major objections. First, we cannot abstract extension from colour, so we cannot hold that the object has colour but no extension no matter how small the object is. His conclusion is that the distinction cannot be sustained. To banish colour, sound, smell and taste (in the non-power senses) from external objects is to banish extension and the other primary qualities as well. Since we have already discussed his rejection of abstraction, we need not consider this argument here.

Berkeley's second objection is that the relativity arguments that presumably show that secondary qualities have an inferior status apply equally to primary qualities. Locke argues that, when we grind porphyry, the sensible colour changes from red to grey or black, even though the stone and the resulting mass of dust are both extended. Similarly when we put a warm and a cold hand in tepid water, the warm hand feels cold and the cold hand feels warm. Since these sensations are incompatible, Locke argues that they cannot both resemble the water's property of temperature. Berkeley holds that if we examine the matter closely, the same relativity occurs with respect to shape and size. A stone looks bigger as we move closer to it and smaller as we move away. Thus, even though it appears extended in both cases, the specific extension we perceive changes and we have no way of knowing which resembles the real size. Shape is also relative. A tabletop appears to have different shapes as we move around it and a coin looks round and elliptical when viewed from different directions. Again we are at a loss to say which appearance resembles the real shape.

This seems to show that *none* of our ideas can be resemblances of physical objects. No set of ideas provides more insight into the physical world than another, so that physical objects, if accepted at all, are reduced to unknown and inexplicable causes. This raises the question of just what Locke means in claiming that only ideas of primary qualities are resemblances. Two theories suggest themselves. First, some interpreters argue that Locke holds that the ideas of size and shape are *generic* resemblances in that, no matter what our position, the physical object always appears to have *some* size and shape even though the specific appearances differ. Reading Locke in this way does not save the theory, however. The sensible colour of porphyry changes as we pound it, but it still has *some* colour, and water has *some* temperature whether warm or cold. The result is that appealing to generic qualities does not point to a difference between the qualities.

The second interpretation (first offered by Maurice Mandlebaum) is that Locke holds that ideas of size, shape, motion, unity and solidity do not resemble the macro qualities of the physical object (i.e. the qualities they have as tables, animals and rocks) any more than the ideas of colour, sound and temperature. Locke's claim is that the ideas of primary qualities at the macro level bear *some* resemblance to the qualities of their ultimate parts. This ties the distinction between primary and secondary qualities to the corpuscular theory. Common-sense objects are composites whose qualities are powers and none of our ideas resemble these qualities. The ideas of extension, shape, solidity and motion, however, resemble the corpuscles making up the objects, if the corpuscular theory is right.

This seems to be Locke's point in the porphyry example. When we grind it, we get smaller and smaller particles with radical changes in the colour and shape of the mass, but at a certain point beyond what we can perceive without microscopical eyes, we would arrive at particles with size and shape, but no colour at all. The example attempts to show how we can come to understand the natural philosopher's claim on the basis of the empiricist theory of how we acquire ideas, that is, by analogy and abstraction (see *Essay*: II viii 19). (Note that in the paragraph immediately before this Locke cites motes and particles seen in sunlight as evidence that there might be even smaller, invisible particles.)

The interpretation is also supported by Locke's text. He says that ideas of secondary qualities "*have no resemblance* of them at all". "There is nothing like our ideas, existing in the bodies themselves"; and later he says that "we plainly discover, that the quality produced, hath commonly no resemblance with anything in the thing producing it; wherefore we look on it as a bare effect of power" (*Essay*: II viii 15, 25). The point seems to be that ideas of primary qualities resemble *something* in the object, even though they fail to resemble the macro qualities. The world of corpuscles is a world of solid, extended particles in motion that in themselves are colourless, soundless, smell-less particles with no temperature.

Berkeley's final criticism is that distinguishing between appearance and reality as Locke does (along with other realists) leads to skepticism. If we do not directly perceive physical objects, we cannot know that they exist, since we are only aware of ideas and cannot demonstrate the real existence of physical objects from them. Berkeley calls this the "twofold existence" theory and offers his theory that physical objects are bundles of ideas as an alternative that avoids skepticism (*PHK*: §86). This is Berkeley's most serious criticism. We shall consider it in Chapter 6 in connection with the problem of empiricism and skepticism.

Summary

In this chapter, we have:

- explained and criticized Berkeley's main arguments for idealism;
- argued that his idealism is consistent with empiricism and suggested that he does not have to assume God's existence to defend it;
- discussed Locke's views on abstraction, substance and primary and secondary qualities and Berkeley's objections.

three

Induction and Hume's empiricism

Hume's *Treatise* and first *Enquiry*

Hume's philosophy is a continuation of Locke. Locke rejects Descartes's claim that there are ideas that "reside within us" and provide the materials for *a priori* knowledge about reality, but accepts his conception of reason. Hume's aim in his first book, *A Treatise of Human Nature* (1739–40), was to extend Locke's programme to reason itself. Although he gives reason a place in mathematics, he rejects it in empirical matters. All reasoning about real existence, he holds, is based on habits established by the association of ideas from experience, or, as we would put it today, on conditioning. The power to form habits is *custom* and non-human animals are governed by a similar principle. Just as Locke attempts to explain ideas by experience and the innate capacity of abstraction, Hume tries to explain inferences about matters of fact by experience and the innate principle of custom. Whereas Locke natural-

---

Hume's wit

'Hume' is the Scottish spelling of Hume's name. His brother, John, changed it to the English 'Home' (although it is pronounced the same way), but Hume refused to change it because of his Scottish nationalism. In his will, he left John a bottle of port and six dozen more on condition that (a) he drink the bottle in two sittings and (b) attest to it in his own hand over the signature 'John Hume'. David Hume said that this would end the only two differences he ever had with his brother on non-religious matters (Mossner 2001: 599).

ized ideas, Hume attempts to naturalize empirical inference by making human reasoning an extension of "animal reasoning".

One way to describe Hume's theory is that he reduces reason (Descartes's "intellect") to the imagination. Descartes holds that the imagination includes perception and memory, and creates associations. Sensory ideas are stored in memory and become associated, but this knowledge is restricted to particular facts and low-level generalizations. Reason then considers this material in the light of its innate ideas and develops natural science based on arithmetic and geometry. It also contains the will, which has the power to withhold assent until we have clear and distinct ideas and certain knowledge. Descartes thinks these are not functions of the body like the imagination, and derive directly from God. Hume's project is to explain knowledge of the world on the basis of the imagination alone, that is, perception, memory and the instinct to connect ideas. He also denies that we are free to withhold assent. The best we can do when experience leads us to believe something is to consider the issue in light of other things we believe from experience. This capacity to view things from a wider perspective is what distinguishes the *wise* from the *vulgar*, not an independent intellectual faculty.

Hume explains his aims and approach in the introduction to the *Treatise*. He says that philosophy cannot advance until we develop a science of human nature, since this is "the only solid foundation for the other sciences". We must become "thoroughly acquainted with the extent and force of human understanding", and explain the nature of our ideas and "the operations of the understanding". He lays down three principles that will guide him (*Treatise*: xvi–xvii).

First, the foundations of this science "must be laid on experience and observation". It must be an "experimental philosophy" in the tradition of Francis Bacon and, although he does not explicitly say so, apparently similar to the natural science developed by Robert Boyle and Isaac Newton. Since the essence of mind is as unknown to us as the essence of external objects, "it must be equally impossible to form any notion of its powers and qualities otherwise than from careful and exact experiments, and the observation of those particular effects, which result from its different circumstances and situations" (*ibid.*).

Secondly, we must offer the widest possible generalizations experience will allow on the fewest basic principles. Or, as he puts it, we must "render all our principles as general as possible, by tracing up our experiments to the utmost, and explaining all effects from the simplest and fewest causes" (*ibid.*).

Thirdly, we must refrain from "any hypothesis, that pretends to discover the ultimate original qualities of human nature". Such explanations go beyond experience and ought to be "rejected as presumptuous and chimerical" (*ibid.*).

Two comments. First, some critics argue that Hume's proposal to determine the boundaries of knowledge empirically is circular and hence that an epistemic theory must be *a priori*. But this is also circular, since we cannot have an *a priori* theory without making assumptions about the epistemic status of the *a priori*. An *a priori* approach is acceptable only if the *a priori* is taken as unproblematic, and Hume is not willing to do this. Moreover, Hume's view is more subtle than it appears. He holds that no theory can be assumptionless. His "experimental" generalizations are based on common sense, or, as he calls it, "common life". The results can then be modified from within, but the project itself has no external justification: "we can give no reason for our most general and most refined principles, beside our experience of their reality". This is "a defect" of all the sciences and arts from "the schools of the philosophers" to "the shops of the meanest artizan" (*Treatise*: *Intro.* xviii). We cannot go beyond common life or "the reason of the mere vulgar" without violating the third rule and speculating about ultimate principles. Hume makes no claim to show that appealing to experience is reliable, but only claims to describe our practice.

This leads to a second point. If his science of human nature is purely descriptive, it is difficult to see how it has a bearing on questions of evidence. Such questions are normative and epistemic theories that address them offer evaluations that go beyond simply describing how people think. This is a problem for any epistemology, empiricist or rationalist. We shall have more to say about it later, but Hume's answer is briefly that the study of evidence and "just reasoning" tells us how to maximize true beliefs. Hence if we want to be wise and satisfy our curiosity about the world, we should learn which modes of reasoning lead to true beliefs.

Hume's theory is based on Berkeley's principle that some ideas are forced on us. He calls such ideas 'impressions' and reserves the term 'ideas' for fainter perceptions that occur when we recall impressions. The more general class is *perceptions*. *Impressions* are distinguished from *ideas* in being stronger and more vivid. He holds three principles: all ideas are copies of impressions; ideas become more lively and have more influence on other ideas by being conjoined with other ideas; and to believe that something exists is itself to have a lively idea that approaches an impression in vividness. When we experience *A* and *B* conjoined, the ideas of *A* and *B* become associated. Then, when an instance of *A* occurs, it causes us to have a lively idea of *B*, that is, the belief that it will occur. If an impression of *B* occurs, the habit is strengthened. On the other hand, if we experience *B*, the idea of *A* is suggested and we believe that *B* was caused by an occurrence of *A*. This process of habit formation is *custom*. In Book I of the *Treatise*, he uses these principles to explain the operation of the understanding. In Books II and III, they are used to explain emotions and moral beliefs.

Unfortunately, Hume's programme was a failure. His appeal to experience is restricted to reflection on his own mental life and the observation of others. By experiments in the *Treatise*, he does not mean active manipulations of the environment, but passive observations. The result is that his science of human nature is not a scientific psychology in the modern sense, but an imaginative natural history of the mind. It is introspective and speculative, what is often referred to derisively as "armchair psychology". His remarks, although often acute, are swamped by what now seems to be naive psychological theorizing. Some admirers take him to be a precursor of cognitive psychology, but this does not make the work less speculative.

Hume's theory is also more ambitious than Locke's, perhaps even heroic. Locke offered his account of ideas as a possible alternative to Descartes's; he did not attempt to prove it by "experiment", but restricted himself to showing how we might explain ideas by experience. Hume wants to show that our beliefs about the world are derived from experience, association and custom. Whereas Locke only claims to be an "under-labourer" clearing out the rubbish so science can proceed, Hume takes himself to be a master builder. The result is that, when it seems that some belief or set of beliefs cannot be explained on his theory, Hume is forced to invent some explanation based on anecdotal evidence from common sense; that is, he is forced to speculate on the slimmest evidence.

The *Treatise* was also a failure in another way. By his own admission, he was unable to explain plausibly how we come to have certain beliefs we all agree we have. The two most famous examples are our beliefs about external objects and personal identity over time. In the case of personal identity, he argues that we have no direct awareness of an enduring self or soul (*Treatise*: I iv 6). The self is as hidden from us as external physical objects. When we try to introspect it, all we find, he says, is another perception and never the self. This is reasonable enough as an epistemic claim, but Hume's goal is to explain how custom and association *cause* the belief that we are the same over time. His theory is that we feign identity based on the similarity of our ideas over time, but, as he admits in the Appendix, this is not so much an explanation as a rejection of the datum to be explained. Our belief in identity turns out to be a pseudo belief. The problem is that he fails to distinguish the psychological question of how we come to have the belief from the epistemic question of whether it is justified. His epistemic sense tells him that belief in identity over time is not reasonable, since we are not directly aware of an enduring self. (Note that this is directly opposed to Berkeley's view that we intuit that we are enduring spiritual substances.) This is a valuable contribution to the debate over whether we have evidence of a soul and one Hume is justly famous for. But it is not an explanation of how we arrive at the belief.

His discussion of belief in external physical objects has the same defect (*Treatise*: I iv 2). He discusses three theories and finds none of them acceptable. They are: (i) the common-sense theory that we directly perceive them; (ii) Berkeley's theory that physical objects are dependent on thought; and (iii) the double-existence theory favoured by Locke and Descartes. Briefly his view on these is as follows.

(i) The first agrees with common sense that we directly perceive physical objects that have both a "continu'd existence" and an independent one. But Hume thinks experience is against it. Illusions show that we are not always directly aware of physical objects. If we press the eye, we have a double image of nearby objects, say, of the cup on the table. That is, we are directly aware of two cups, and, if the first theory is true, this means that there are two cups, but this is not what we believe.

(ii) The second theory holds that physical objects are Berkeleyan ideas forced on us in coherent patterns, while "things" like the second cup are illusory or aberrant ideas. Hume thinks this is a natural extension of the popular theory, but holds that we cannot believe it. We may say we do (as Berkeley did, although Hume does not name him), but Hume thinks this is disingenuous. As soon as we leave our studies, we fall back into the vulgar system that physical objects are both directly perceived and independent existences, without being able to explain illusions such as double images. As he says in the *Enquiry Concerning Human Understanding*, "Nature is always too strong for principle" (*EHU*: XII ii 160).

(iii) This leads to the theory of double existence. This holds that perceptions (i.e. the direct objects of perception) are mind dependent, but that physical objects are independent of mind. This is philosophically the most sophisticated theory, since it draws a distinction between perceptions as appearances and their objects as realities. But Hume also finds it unacceptable. Since we are only aware of perceptions, we cannot discover anything about physical objects independently of them. Just as an idea gets in the way when we try to find the self, so ideas get in the way when we try to find physical objects. The most we can say about them is that they cause our perceptions; in other words, we can only have a relative idea of them (in the sense discussed above in § "The idea of substance" (p. 46)), but we cannot give any further content to them as causes. Hume thinks this makes the double-existence theory incoherent. It claims that physical objects are independent of perceptions, then gives further perceptions to explain what they are like. It is "over-and-above loaded with this absurdity, that it at once denies and establishes the vulgar supposition" (*Treatise*: I iv 2, 218).

As in the case of personal identity, it is not clear what Hume is doing. Is he giving a psychological account of the causes of belief in external objects or defending a philosophical theory of what we should believe about them? He seems to assume that theories cannot be acceptable to common sense if there are good grounds for disbelieving them, but this over-rationalizes the common man. There might be psychological causes for believing what reflection reveals to be untenable; there is no reason for thinking that the psychological underpinning of our beliefs reflects what we should believe.

One interpretation is that this part of the *Treatise* is not aimed at defending positive theories about the issues or about the psychological basis of our beliefs, but has a purely negative function. Hume is trying to show that Cartesian reason ('pure reason' as opposed to reason based on custom) fails to justify acceptable alternatives to what we naturally believe, that is, our "vulgar" opinions. As a result, it can only lead to doubts we cannot resolve and that we cannot live with when we leave our studies. If this is right, this group of sections (*Treatise*: I iv) is part of one master argument against the adequacy of pure reason on both philosophical and psychological grounds.

Even if we ignore these problems and concentrate on Hume's theory as a non-psychological epistemology theory, the project was a failure. Hume was too Lockean to accept Berkeley's conclusions, but too close to Berkeley to make a sharp distinction between the internal and external worlds that would have allowed him to give content to his naturalism.

Whatever we think of the *Treatise*, it was clearly a failure in Hume's eyes. He hoped to make his reputation with it, but, as he said, it fell still born from the presses. Rather than rewriting it or producing a second edition, he set out to make his writing style more accessible (more "engaging", as he said). His solution was to write shorter pieces that fit together to support an overall view and forego any attempt to sum up his position in another tome like the *Treatise*. The result is that his later writings keep the psychology to a minimum and concentrate on the criteria of "just reasoning". In the *Enquiry Concerning Human Understanding*, Section I, he calls this "mental geography". This is not psychology, but a description of the distinguishing marks of knowledge and belief, and the quality of the evidence for beliefs. He defends empiricism and offers rules for causal reasoning and testimony in order to establish the boundaries between superstition and reasonable belief. His aim, in other words, is to give criteria so we may "reason justly" about the world. The result is that the *Enquiry* is the second great defence of empiricism in the British tradition (after Locke's *Essay*).

The defence of empiricism

The *Enquiry* has traditionally been taken to be a watered-down version of the *Treatise*. Under the influence of Kant, nineteenth-century interpreters held that Hume rewrote the simpler parts of the *Treatise* as a series of essays in the tradition of "easy philosophy", as he put it in the first section, in order to gain a public. More recent work rejects this interpretation. First, although Hume refers to easy and difficult philosophy in Section I, he does not suggest that he will pursue the easy kind. He says just the opposite. He says that the public will always prefer easy philosophy, but that it is necessary to do hard philosophy in order to advance the subject. If we refrain from doing it, we leave superstition in charge of its own retreat whereas philosophy should pursue it into the woods and destroy it. He clearly takes mental geography to be difficult philosophy that is necessary if we are to distinguish between justified and unjustified belief. In the last section (Section XII), he offers a classification of the major disciplines based on his empiricism. Any treatise that does not contain abstract reasonings concerning relations of ideas (e.g. mathematics and geometry) or reasonings concerning matters of fact (such as history and natural philosophy) ought to be committed "to the flames", since "it can contain nothing but sophistry and illusion" (*Enquiry*: XII iii, 165).

Secondly, a careful reading of the *Enquiry* shows that the essays form an integrated pattern. The twelve sections fall into four groups of three essays each. The first three groups have two longer essays followed by a shorter section that provides a transition to the next group. The only exception is the last group, which has a long section that is the conclusion. This discusses skepticism and suggests rules for reasoning as "a wise man" (see key point "Organization of Hume's *Enquiry Concerning Human Understanding*"). We shall concentrate on his defence of empiricism in Sections IV and V and his theory of the causal relation in Section VIII. His relation to skepticism will be discussed in Chapter 6 and his criticisms of religious belief in Chapter 7.

Hume's empiricism is based on his distinction between the kinds of propositions. A *relation of ideas* is a proposition whose negation is a contradiction, while a *matter of fact* does not have to be true, but can be denied without contradiction. Relations of ideas can be known *a priori*, while matters of fact can only be known empirically. Some examples are:

(1) Triangles are three-sided figures.
(2) All mothers are parents.
(3) All mothers love their children.
(4) The internal angles of a triangle equal 180 degrees.
(5) $e = mc^2$
(6) Bread causes nourishment.
(7) Hamlet exists.
(8) God exists.
(9) Four-sided triangles exist.

The first two are relations of ideas since triangles that are not three-sided and mothers who are not parents are contradictory. Proposition (3) is a matter of fact, since we cannot tell from the concept of a mother that all mothers love their children. To know whether they all do or not we must look to nature. That the internal angles of a triangle are 180 degrees (i.e. proposition (4)) is a relation of ideas, since denying it implies a contradiction, even though we cannot tell that it is true by looking up the meaning of 'triangle' in the dictionary. In this, it differs from the first two, which lead immediately to contradictions if they are denied. Proposition (5) is a matter of fact, since energy is not by definition equal to the product of mass and the square of the speed of light; physicists had to discover it by observation. Proposition (6) also is a matter of fact.

The last three are existential propositions. Propositions (7) and (8) are matters of fact, according to Hume. 'Hamlet exists', which happens to be false, can only be known by experience since there is nothing contradictory about his not existing. Hume makes the same claim about God's existence. He may or may not exist, but we cannot know whether he does simply by knowing the meaning of the term. In this, Hume follows Locke (and Berkeley) in rejecting *a priori* arguments that he exists.

Proposition (9) is a special case. That four-sided triangles exist is clearly false and so is not a relation of ideas; it is also not a matter of fact, but a contradiction – it cannot possibly be true. This shows that Hume's categories of relations of ideas and matters of fact are not exhaustive. There is a third category: contradictions that are neither true by definition nor go beyond the meanings of the terms, but are contradictions as they stand. The three categories are:

- relations of ideas   must be true   necessary truths
- contradictories   must be false   necessary falsehoods
- matters of fact   may be true or false non-conceptual propositions

A convenient term for matters of fact is 'contingent'. A *contingent* proposition's truth-value depends on the way the world is and is not true (or false) on only conceptual grounds.

Hume explains his empiricism in these terms. He holds that all existential truths are matters of fact and can only be known empirically. He sums up his view at the end of the *Enquiry*. He says that the abstract sciences (arithmetic and geometry) deal with quantity and number, and are capable of demonstration. They rest ultimately on the meanings of the terms and, if there is any indecision about their claims, "it proceeds entirely from the undeterminate meaning of words, which is corrected by juster definitions" (*EHU*: XII iii 163). The propositions of such sciences are relations of ideas and can be known *a priori*. All other human enquiries "regard only matter of fact and existence", and are incapable of demonstration. Hume continues:

> Whatever *is* may *not be*. No negation of a fact can involve a contradiction. The non-existence of any being, without exception, is as clear and distinct an idea as its existence. The proposition, which affirms it not to be, however false, is no less conceivable and intelligible, than that which affirms it to be.
>
> (*EHU*: XII iii 164)

In the abstract sciences, every false proposition is "confused and unintelligible" and "can never be distinctly conceived". On the other hand, that Caesar or the archangel Gabriel never existed may be false, "but still is perfectly conceivable, and implies no contradiction". These are based on reasoning about cause and effect, and causal arguments "are founded entirely on experience".

> If we reason *a priori*, anything may appear able to produce anything. The falling of a pebble may, for aught we know, extinguish the sun; or the wish of a man control the planets in their orbits. It is only experience, which teaches us the nature and bounds of cause and effect, and enables us to infer the existence of one object from that of another. (*EHU*: XII iii 164)

Hume's argument for this is found in *Enquiry*:

(1) Statements of real existence are matters of fact.
(2) All matters of fact beyond present experience are based on arguments from cause and effect.
(3) Such arguments are never *a priori*.
Thus (4) No knowledge of real existence is *a priori*, but "arises entirely from experience, when we find that any particular objects are constantly conjoined with each other" (*EHU* IV i 27).

Hume puts forward the conclusion "as a general proposition, which admits of no exception". The key premises are (2) and (3). Let us consider them in turn.

Why does all reasoning beyond present experience rest on causal beliefs? He cites two examples as evidence. First, if you ask why a man believes his friend is not in the country, he might tell you that the friend said he was going away and he is a man of his word, or that he just received a letter from him from France, both of which depend on causal knowledge. Secondly, when we hear a voice in the dark we are sure another person is present because we know that such sounds are typically made by human beings. This is not very convincing. Two examples do not support a conclusion about *all* existential claims. A more theoretical reason is needed, and what is this? The answer lies in Hume's account of our knowledge of physical objects. He holds that objects that have real existence must have duration and be independent of what we individually think about them. But we cannot know this from present experience. All this tells us is that the object exists now; it does not tell us that it exists when we close our eyes or look away, or that it is independent of our present thought. To know this, we must take the present experience to be a sign of an enduring object. If we put a log on the fire and come back later to find it has turned to embers, we infer that it existed in the interval because that is what happens to burning logs. Our present experience and memory convinces us that the log is real and not an aberrant idea unconnected with other perceptions we could have had if we had been in the room, and this general knowledge rests on generalizations about causes and effects.

It might be argued (as Berkeley did) that we can tell the difference between an illusion and a genuine perception directly, since our ideas are more vivid and detailed when the object is real. But even here we need background beliefs. We would have to know that vivid and detailed perceptions are signs of real objects and this can only be discovered by experience. As children, we learn to distinguish between dreaming and perceiving by appealing to the coherence of our perceptions and coherence relations can only be discovered by experience. This is Hume's more general argument for (2). We shall have more to say about it later.

Hume has two arguments for premise (3), that is, that knowledge of causes and effects is empirical. The more general one is suggested by Hume's remark that, for all we know *a priori*, the falling of a pebble may be followed by the planets wavering in their orbits. Causal propositions have the form *Every φ is ψ* and are not relations of ideas. If they were, there would be a logical link between the subject and predicate that would allow us to know them *a priori* (as there is in the case of 'Every mother is a parent'). Since there is no logical link, causal propositions are matters of fact and cannot be known *a priori*.

Hume also gives a second, more elaborate argument. We know that if a moving billiard ball hits a stationary one, the moving ball will stop and the other will move. We might think that if we were brought into the world suddenly and shown one ball moving towards the other, we could predict what would happen. But Hume says that this prediction "must be entirely arbitrary" since the prior and subsequent events are entirely distinct. Considered *a priori*, any number of events can be imagined as following the first and any choice we make from them would be arbitrary. By 'arbitrary' here he means that the inference would not be rationally justified, but would be a guess and have no claim to being "just reasoning". This would be so even if we guessed correctly. We would be right "by accident" and have no rational basis for the belief. "Why then should we give the preference to one, which is no more consistent or conceivable than the rest? All our reasonings *a priori* will never be able to show us any foundation for this preference" (*EHU*: IV i 30).

It is important to note that Hume's argument is normative. 'Just reasoning', 'entirely arbitrary' and being right 'by accident' are not descriptive, but refer to norms of acceptable reasoning. Hume holds that a rational person would not feel a rational obligation to accept an *a priori* argument for a matter of fact (such as that ψ will occur after φ), but would demand an argument based on the conjunction of φ and ψ in the past. Hume says that the conclusion of the general argument for empiricism, that is, (4), is a generalization, but a generalization about the standards accepted by those who have reflected carefully on the matter, by the *wise*, as he puts it, and not by the *vulgar*, where 'wise' and 'vulgar' are used normatively.

The problem of induction

There are two questions about causation: the basis of our knowledge of causal laws and the nature of causation itself. We shall consider the first in this section and the second in the next.

As we saw, Hume holds that causal relations cannot be known *a priori* since causal laws are not relations of ideas. They must be known from experience. We know that eating bread has always been followed by "nourishment and support" and so expect that it will in the future. But we cannot infer bread's secret power of nourishing us from its sensible qualities since there is no known connection between the outward appearances and its power to nourish. We must infer its causal power from our experience of human beings being nourished when they eat it. But this only tells us what we have experienced in the past and not why this "should be extended to future times." We have two propositions – eating bread in the past has been followed by nourishment, and eating bread in the future will also be followed by nourishment – and we cannot intuit any connection between them. Hume thinks the inference rests on the principle that "like causes will be followed by like effects". But this is itself a matter of fact and, if empiricism is correct, must be based on experience and we can do this only by assuming it, which is circular. As Hume says, "all our experimental conclusions proceed upon the supposition, that the future will be conformable to the past" and to prove this "must be evidently going in a circle, and taking that for granted, which is the very point at issue" (*EHU*: IV ii 35–6).

The problem is inferring universal statements from limited information. We must assume that unexamined instances will resemble examined ones. We may call this the *inductive principle*. Hume's argument is this:

(1) The inductive principle is either a relation of ideas or a matter of fact.

(2) It is not a relation of ideas, since its negation is not a contradiction.

Thus (3) It is a matter of fact.

(4) All justification of matters of fact beyond the present rests on the principle.

Thus (5) It can be justified only if we suppose it is true, which is arguing in a circle.

Thus (6) It cannot be justified.

This is known as *the problem of induction* and sometimes as *Hume's problem*. What are we to make of it? The most vulnerable premise is (4). Why should we believe that all non-*a priori* knowledge rests on induction? That it does seems to rest on empiricism and why should we accept this? Unfortunately, it is not as simple as this. Premise (4) does not rest on his empiricism; it is rather that his empiricism rests on premise (4). The reason is that even if you hold that there is *a priori* knowledge of real existence, there is still no way of justifying matter-of-fact generalizations from experience without assuming the principle. As a result, premise (4) is accepted by both empiricists and rationalists. A rationalist might argue that the principle is justified *a priori*, but this shifts the problem to showing just how it is justified *a priori*. Furthermore, Hume says, the argument must be simple enough for children and non-philosophers to understand it.

Several points should be noted about the problem. First, it is some-times taken to be an objection to Hume's empiricism. Hume, however, thinks it cannot be solved and takes it to be a central lesson of empiri-cism. Furthermore, he holds that it is a problem for any theory of knowl-edge and challenges those who disagree to offer a solution. He thinks it shows that knowledge beyond the present rests on an assumption we cannot discharge in a way that will "satisfy our reason". He calls this conclusion a "skeptical doubt". Whether it leads to skepticism depends on what you mean by 'skepticism'. If you hold that the problem commits us to abstaining from reasoning from the past to the future, he is not a skeptic, since he thinks we cannot refrain from making such infer-ences. If you take 'skepticism' to mean that we cannot be *certain* about any beliefs beyond the present, he is a skeptic, but thinks that this is not a serious form of skepticism. (As we shall see later, this is better called 'fallibilism'.) He is also a skeptic if you take 'skepticism' to mean that knowledge cannot rest on an unjustified assumption. But he does not take this to imply that there is no distinction between just and unjust reasoning. He thinks that justified reasoning in common life is relative to the assumption that induction is reliable (as well as perception and memory). The most he will admit to is a "mitigated skepticism", which recommends that we avoid dogmatism and enquiry into matters beyond our comprehension, such as providing non-circular justification of our faculties. We shall return to this topic in Chapter 6.

Secondly, it might be thought that Hume's argument only applies to inferences to universal propositions and not to probability judgements. But this is a mistake. If we know that 60 per cent of patients with a cer-tain ailment die and infer that there is a 0.6 probability that this patient will die, we are still assuming the inductive principle. We are inferring that because 60 per cent have died in the past, the same percentage will die in the future. This shows that any inference from examined to unex-amined cases rests on the inductive principle, whether the conclusion is a universal or a probability statement.

Thirdly, it might be argued that Hume's practice refutes his doubts, since he continues to act on induction. He says that this mistakes the purpose of his question. "As an agent, I am quite satisfied in the point; but as a philosopher, who has some share of curiosity, I will not say scepticism, I want to learn the foundation of this inference." Nothing he has read or discovered has removed the difficulty and, if no solution can be found, we will at least "be sensible of our ignorance, if we do not augment our knowledge" (*EHU*: IV ii 38).

Hume's "skeptical solution"

Hume's positive view is that we follow induction instinctively and not because intellect sanctions it. As a result, inductive reasoning is unaffected by our inability to justify it (*EHU*: V i). When we experience events conjoined, "we are determined by custom alone to expect the one from the appearance of the other". This is common to the higher animals and is "the great guide of human life". Without it "we should be entirely ignorant of every matter of fact beyond what is immediately present to the memory or the senses" and "should never know how to adjust means to ends" or how to produce any effect (*EHU*: V i 43–5).

It is sometimes thought that appealing to instinct leaves no room for reasoning and the control of belief, but this is not Hume's view. He distinguishes between inferences and reasonings. An *inference* occurs when the mind passes from one perception to another automatically without thought, while *reasoning* is based on premises and is subject to control. Neither can be shown to be reliable by reasoning, but this does not mean that lesser principles and beliefs are not subject to control by argument. Our trust in external perception and memory is also instinctual. The principles involved in these cases are (i) what we spontaneously believe on the basis of perception has some likelihood of being true and (ii) what we seem to remember has some intrinsic credibility (*Treatise*: I iv 7, 265). Both processes are needed for induction. We cannot make inferences from examined instances unless we have observed them and remember having done so. Furthermore, there is no way to confirm the reliability of perception except by further observation, which begs the question. We can test the reliability of one sense modality by means of others, but only if we assume its reliability somewhere else. The same is true of memory. We cannot justify memory by going back to the past, and pitting one memory belief against another. We can only confirm it locally by assuming it elsewhere.

The main problem with Hume's theory is his theory of belief. He holds that beliefs differ from imagined ideas or fictions in being more vivid and forceful. My idea of Gideon is more vivid when I believe that he exists than when I think he is just a figment, but otherwise the idea is the same in both cases. He uses this account to explain how custom works. After we have come to associate the two events in the billiard-ball case and have an impression of one moving towards the other, our idea of what will follow next is enlivened because of the association and we believe that the moving ball will transfer its motion to the other ball.

This clearly fails as an account of belief. People with lively imaginations can have more vivid ideas of what they imagine than of what they perceive. Their idea of the sun on an overcast day when they believe it is daylight may be less vivid than their idea when they imagine it at night, even though they do not believe it is daylight. To believe that the sun is shining is to accept the proposition that it is, while to imagine that it is is to consider the proposition without accepting it. The idea is the same in both cases; whether we believe it or not depends on our attitude towards it. It may be difficult to give an account of this state of mind and ultimately we might have to take it to be unanalysable, but the difference does not lie in the quality of the idea, as Hume claims.

Hume was led to this view by his difficulty in explaining the idea of existence. Locke held that when we believe that Caesar exists, we assent to the agreement between the ideas of Caesar and the idea of existence, that is, we assent to the proposition that he exists. Hume thinks we have no idea of existence distinct from that of Caesar in this case; we only have one idea, that of Caesar (*Treatise*: I i 6). This is also the only idea we have in mind, when we wonder whether he existed (and is not just an historical fiction); hence the difference between believing and imagining must lie in the quality of the idea.

He may have derived this view from Berkeley. As we saw, Berkeley held that the difference between a real and an imagined thing is that the idea of a real thing is forced on us while the idea of an imagined thing is not. In any case, the idea of existence is an abstract idea. If we hold that all ideas are images and there are no abstract ideas, we are going to have trouble explaining existential beliefs.

The first clear account of existence propositions derives from the logic of C. S. Peirce (1839–1914) and Gottlob Frege (1848–1925) in the nineteenth century. They hold that '*F* exists' can be analysed as *Something is F* or equivalently as *There is an F*, while '*F*s do not exist' can be read as *Nothing is F* or *It is not the case that something is F*. To believe that there are *F*s is to accept the proposition that there are, while to wonder whether there are is to consider the proposition without accepting it (to entertain it, as we say). This still leaves the notion of what it is to accept propositions unexplained. A useful preliminary account is that to accept a proposition is to be willing to use it as a premise in reasoning or as a reason for action. This explains acceptance in terms of its consequences for behaviour, but it is not strictly a behaviourist theory. It takes belief to be a mental state that has certain effects on our "logical" behaviour as reasoning beings and on our overt behaviour as agents. More needs to be said to make it an acceptable theory, but that

> ### *"I'm no epicure"*
> Later in life, Hume prided himself on his cooking skills and had an extensive collection of French recipes. His dinners were so famous in Scotland that a wit said that the Edinburgh *Literati* should be called the *Eaterati*. But Hume always insisted he was not a gourmet. He told a friend, "Ye ken I'm no epicure, only a glutton" (Mossner 2001: 560–61).

is a question for the philosophy of mind and psychology. Regardless of the details, it does account for the difference between believing that Caesar exists and wondering whether he does: to believe it is to have a certain disposition we do not have when we simply consider it.

Hume is more successful when dealing with universal propositions. He holds that to believe that bread nourishes is to associate the idea of bread with the idea of nourishment, that is, to have a habit relating the ideas. Unlike 'Caesar exists', where there is only one idea, here we have two distinct ideas that we associate. Thus, if we perceive bread, we expect to be nourished if we eat it or, in Hume's language, the impression of the bread will be followed by the idea of nourishment. A simpler example is 'All burgundies are red'. If all the burgundies you have experienced have been red, you will believe this by *induction*. Then, if you order a burgundy, you will expect a red wine, and if the people at the next table are drinking a red wine, you might infer that it is a burgundy. In the first case, we have a deduction and in the second an inference to a hypothesis. If the proposition is a causal one, *deduction* is inference from cause to effect and *hypothesis* (or abduction) is inference from effect to cause. The first is valid while the second only offers some likelihood that the hypothesis is true. The psychological process corresponding to deduction and hypothesis may be called *suggestion*, while the process by which the habit is formed is *association*. We shall say more about these three modes of inference in Chapter 5.

The nature of causation

Hume holds that there is no necessary connection between cause and effect. If there were, '*A* causes *B*' would be a relation of ideas and we would be able to tell by examining the cause that the effect will occur. But it is always possible to deny a causal statement without contradiction. Consider the billiard-ball example. If there were a necessary connection between cause and effect, we could tell what would happen simply by observing the moving ball approaching the stationary one. But we cannot, so the statement that the moving ball will stop and transfer the motion to the stationary one cannot be a relation of ideas and the law that this will happen cannot assert a necessary tie between the events. All we are aware of, according to Hume, is that the supposed cause precedes the effect, is contiguous with it and that the events occur together when we observe them repeatedly. He concludes that the idea of cause contains only these three ideas: priority, succession and conjunction, and no necessary connection. He offers two definitions of cause.

C1: "… we may define a cause to be *an object, followed by another, and where all the objects, similar to the first are followed by objects similar to the second*". He adds that this means: "*where, if the first object had not been, the second never have existed*".

C2: We may also call a cause "*an object followed by another, and whose appearance always conveys the thought to that other*" (*EHU*: VII ii 76–7).

C1 reduces the supposed necessary connection between the cause and effect to a constant conjunction. C2 explains it in terms of our habit of inferring the effect from the cause when we have experienced the conjunction in the past. C1 is the *truth-condition* for A causing B and C2 may be called the *assertion-condition*. C1 tells us that 'A causes B' is *true* when the events are constantly conjoined and C2 that we *assert* that A causes B, when experience has led us to associate them so that when we experience an instance of A, we expect B to occur also.

Hume thinks that C2 explains why we think of causation as a form of necessity. After a man has experienced what happens to the billiard balls, he will say that the events are connected. The reason is that "he now *feels* these events to be *connected* in his imagination". When we say that one event is connected with another, "we mean only, that they have acquired a connexion in our thought" (*ibid*.). Hume puts the point psychologically, but it can also be put in terms of logic. If we associate bread with nourishment and see bread, we will infer that it is nourishing and say that it *must* be nourishing. The argument is:

> Bread nourishes.
> This is bread.
> Thus This is nourishing.

This is valid and the conclusion necessarily follows from the premises: given the premises, the conclusion *must* be true. The necessity is not a connection between bread and nourishment, but between the premises and the conclusion. Talk of necessity reflects the logical character of the argument and does not assert a tie in reality. We experience only the constant conjunction and "as we *feel* a customary connexion between the ideas, we transfer that feeling to the objects". Hume adds that nothing is more usual than for us "to apply to external bodies every internal sensation, which they occasion" (*EHU*: VII ii 78n.).

This suggests that Hume thinks necessary connection is an illusion, but he also says it is the central component of the ordinary idea of causation and sometimes writes as if there are necessary connections in nature. Several theories have been offered to explain his view.

The dominant interpretation in the twentieth century was that he rejects necessity completely on the grounds that we cannot observe any connection. We have impressions of the events, but none of the connection. Hence we can have no idea of it and it must be meaningless. This interprets Hume as holding that the claim of a necessary connection cannot be verified and is meaningless. The logical positivists of the mid-twentieth century favoured this interpretation and took Hume to be a founder of their movement. We may call this the *Old Hume*.

More recently, Hume has been read as holding that there is a necessary connection, but that we can only conjecture that it exists and cannot frame a clear idea of its nature. This reading coincides with the resurgence of realism in the latter part of the twentieth century and has been called the *New Hume*.

Both interpretations seek to explain Hume's view that the necessary-connection theory lacks content. The first holds that it has no content whatsoever and is useless for understanding causation, since it is unverifiable. The second holds that it has enough content for us to presume that there is a connection, even though we cannot explain it in detail. Perhaps we have a relative idea of it (like Locke's relative idea of substratum), but we cannot give a coherent and fully satisfying account of it.

A third interpretation is that Hume rejects the connection, as the verificationist interpretation claims, but not on the grounds that it is unverifiable. Rather he thinks that positing it is a non-theory and hopelessly obscure, because we cannot explain how it differs from accidental conjunction, on the one hand, and a logically necessary relation, on the other. He does not reject it on epistemic grounds, that is, that we cannot observe or know it, but on the grounds that it is metaphysically unsound. On this view, Hume holds that only particulars exist and there is no real possibility or necessity in things; the only acceptable modal notions are logical possibility and logical necessity, which depend on convention and stipulated relations between concepts. We may call this the *nominalist* interpretation.

Hume's copy principle is evidence for the verificationist interpretation. He holds that every idea must resemble a corresponding impression, or be a complex idea consisting of components that resemble them. Since impressions are forceful perceptions deriving from sense experience or introspection, words that do not depict ideas deriving from experience are meaningless. Some passages support this interpretation, but they are indecisive, according to New Hume interpreters. In later writings, he uses the copy principle as a method of clarifying ideas: if we are unclear about the meaning of a word, we should look to its corresponding impression. (Recall his use of the billiard-ball example as a model of a causal relation.) If there is no impression, this only means that we cannot clarify the concept, not that there is no concept at all. The fact that he never suggests that there is no concept of God even though we cannot verify his existence is also evidence that he is not a verificationist.

Evidence for the nominalist interpretation can be found in the details of his discussion of causation. He argues that our idea of power (i.e. of possibilities *de re* or in objects) is relative like that of cause itself. A power is "the *unknown* circumstance of an object, by which the degree or quantity of its effect is fixed and determined" and "the effect is the measure of the power" (*EHU*: VII ii 77u.). In other words, we have no idea of a power other than that some feature of the object is constantly conjoined with the effect. If philosophers "had any idea of power, as it is in itself, why could not they measure it in itself"? The causal power of bread to nourish, for example, is nothing more than the fact that when we eat it, we are nourished. We cannot attribute any more reality to it than what comes out in the events conjoined with it.

What is interesting about this interpretation is that it has the same consequence as the verificationist reading, but on different grounds. If Hume is a nominalist, he holds that talk of necessary connection is unacceptable because it is a theory without content. It may seem informative, but this is an illusion. The most we can say about the connection is that it is (i) *more than* just a conjunction of events and (ii) *less than* a logically necessary connection such as we find in a relation of ideas. The nominalist holds, like the positivist, that this is a non-theory and is empty, but not because of our inability to verify the connection. The failure is a theoretical one, not one deriving from lack of knowledge. We have only indicated that necessity in nature is neither (i) nor (ii), and philosophy demands positive clarification and not clarification by negation. But this debate is ongoing and cannot be settled here.

Summary

The main topics discussed in this chapter are:

- Hume's attempt to develop a science of human nature in the *Treatise*;
- his defence of empiricism in the *Enquiry Concerning Human Understanding*;
- the problem of induction and his claim that it cannot be solved;
- his theory of causation itself and the three interpretations of it: the verificationist, realist and nominalist.

Except for the last topic, these are epistemological issues. We will discuss, in Chapter 6, whether his claim that we cannot justify the reliability of induction, perception and memory implies skepticism and, in Chapter 7, his use of empiricism to criticize the rationality of religious belief.

four

Foundations and empiricism

Empirical knowledge has traditionally been viewed as a structure of theories and hypotheses resting on a foundation that provides input from the world. Such a view is called *foundationalism*. This chapter will discuss the main versions of this theory and its alternatives along with Wilfrid Sellars's criticism that traditional versions of the theory rest on a myth.

Foundations and its alternatives

Hume subscribes to a foundations theory. He says that our beliefs carry us beyond memory and the senses, "yet some fact must always be present to the sense or memory, from which we may first proceed in drawing these conclusions". When we learn about past ages from history, we must read the books, inferring one testimony from another "till we arrive at the eye-witnesses and spectators of these distant events". If we did not arrive at some fact present to the senses, "our reasonings would be merely hypothetical, and however the particular links might be connected", the chain of inferences would have "nothing to support it" and we could not "arrive at the knowledge of any real existence" by means of it (*EHU*: V i 45–6).

This requirement derives from the ancient skeptics. They held that there are four possible ways to justify beliefs: They can rest:

- on a *foundation* that is not further justified, as Hume argues;

- on beliefs which in turn rest on others *ad infinitum*, that is, justification must lead to a *regress* of reasons;
- on other beliefs that are ultimately justified by the original beliefs, leading us in a *circle*;
- on beliefs we accept as *assumptions* or on the basis of convention.

The skeptics thought that the first, foundationalism, was the only alternative with any plausibility. The regress theory leaves our reasonings "merely hypothetical", as Hume says, and the appeal to circular justification begs the question. We cannot justify a belief by other beliefs that assume it; no one who doubted the belief would accept an argument that assumes it. Nor can we justify beliefs on assumptions that are not themselves justified. If the premises are simply assumed, the argument is still hypothetical. We have only shown that it is warranted, *if* the assumption is true and have not offered evidence that it is.

These arguments support foundationalism, but the skeptics argued that this cannot be defended either, since any proposal for determining when a proposition is justified in itself is open to challenge and may be mistaken. The result, they argued, is that we cannot adequately support any claim to knowledge and should withhold judgement on whether we have any. This extreme view is skepticism, which we shall examine in Chapter 6. Here we are interested in the argument as a framework for discussing the problem of foundations.

Among the alternatives to foundationalism, the only one to receive extensive support is the appeal to circularity. This holds that beliefs are ultimately justified by being part of a system of beliefs that cohere or support one another. An example is knowledge that we are not dreaming. Since any test to show that we are awake might itself be part of a dream, we cannot prove that we are awake. Defenders of the coherence theory argue that we can know it only because dream beliefs do not cohere with other beliefs. I now believe that I am working at the computer and not just dreaming that I am (as I did last night when I was trying to work out what to write). My reason is that I seem to see the computer, am aware that the lights are on and see the words on the screen, all while I am sitting in my room surrounded by books with the birds chirping outside. Here a number of beliefs support one another, but none of them seems to have any warrant in itself. It is only as a group that they are warranted. Such is the argument of the coherence theory of justification or *coherentism*.

The only plausible form of regress theory holds that justification comes to an end only because we run out of time or patience to respond to skeptical quibbles. The result is that justification is open-ended and is neither circular nor based on a foundation. This might be defensible, but it collapses into the assumption theory. Any chain of reasons that ends arbitrarily or for non-epistemic reasons (like our impatience) justifies the conclusion only on the assumption of the last reason, and, since this is unjustified, we must conclude once again that the justification is "merely hypothetical".

The only serious attempt to hold that observation statements are assumptions is by Karl Popper in the early twentieth century. He held that observation statements in science cannot be justified by experiences, since this confuses justification and psychological considerations. Only propositions can justify beliefs. Justification depends on reasons and logical relations between propositions, not on feelings or sensations. He concluded that observation statements are accepted by scientists as a matter of convention. They *decide* to accept certain ones and not others, and these provide the basis for our rational acceptance and rejection of hypotheses in science (Popper 1968: V §§25, 29).

There is something in Popper's objections to justifying beliefs by appeal to psychological states, that is, to what is called *psychologism* in logic, but he does not say enough about how scientists (or ordinary folk) decide which observation statements to accept. If scientists decide which data their theories are supposed to explain, it is difficult to see how science differs from theology or political ideologies. We cannot simply accept some statements and not others, if the statements are to provide *evidence* for other claims. The beliefs must be based on grounds that have authority independently of our saying that they have authority. As a result, Popper's conventionalist strategy fails to answer Hume's question.

Let us look at Hume's answer. He says that the answer is "a simple one", although it is "pretty remote" from the common theories. "All belief of matter of fact or real existence is derived merely from some object, present to the memory or senses, and a customary conjunction between that and some other object" (*EHU*: V i 46). This is Hume's empiricism. It should be noted that he is not referring to the individual's beliefs at a moment in time. Justification rests on what *he* experiences at the moment and remembers of his past experiences, or by a combination of this and induction. Since the memory must be of past experiences and induction must be based on examined instances, memory and induction presuppose experience, so the foundation, according to Hume, is experience or perception. To put it in his terminology, all knowledge of reality must rest on impressions. When I perceive an apple, I have an impression of a reddish, spherical object, which I take to be evidence of an apple that continues to exist when I am not perceiving it. Impressions here may be taken to be particular ideas in Locke's sense, that is, images, or alternatively as beliefs that we are being appeared to in a certain manner, since he takes a belief to be just a vivid and lively perception and no perceptions are more lively than impressions. But it is useful to distinguish the two accounts, as Locke did. If we do, we can describe the process of acquiring empirical knowledge as follows: we have (i) an idea or sensation of a physical object, then (ii) a belief about the character of this idea, and (iii) finally a further belief about the physical object. It is not clear whether the foundation should be taken to be the sensation or the belief about it. There are also questions about the nature of the sensation and about Berkeley's claim that we are directly aware of the physical object itself or infer it from an idea independent of it.

To clarify these issues, it is useful to consider the foundations theory Russell held in 1912. Russell is not an empiricist in the strict sense (since he holds that we have *a priori* knowledge of real abstract entities), but his theory of empirical knowledge can be taken as an elaboration of the theory of Locke, Hume and, with some modifications, Berkeley. It also provides a background for discussing more recent criticisms of the theory by Sellars and the major issue dividing foundationalist and coherentist theories.

Acquaintance, appearing and the given

Russell distinguishes between *knowledge by acquaintance* and *knowledge by description*. We are acquainted "with anything of which we are directly aware, without the intermediary of any process of inference or any knowledge of truths", and have only descriptive knowledge of things of which we are not directly aware (Russell 1959: 46). People who have seen the pope know him by acquaintance; the rest of us know him indirectly by means of some description such as 'the spiritual leader of the Catholic church'. If we have seen him, we know by acquaintance that the pope exists; otherwise we know it by knowing that some proposition such as 'The spiritual leader of the Catholic Church exists' is true. In the first case, we know he exists because we have seen him; in the second, because we know some description of him. Similarly, we may say that we are acquainted with the table when we see it in the room. But if we are out of the room, we know that it exists only because we know that 'The table in the next room exists' is true.

These examples assume that we directly perceive people and physical objects, but Russell holds that we learn from science that this is not the case. When we view a table from an angle, we are acquainted with a brownish trapezoidal shape, and, when we view it from above, with a lighter coloured rectangular shape (Russell 1959: ch. 1). These are distinct sense data and the table itself is known under the description 'the cause of these sense data'. Similarly those who have seen the pope were acquainted with sense data of him at the time, and know him indirectly as the cause of them; now they know him as the remote cause of those remembered images. Russell's reason for this derives from physics. We know objects because light waves cause images on the retina and eventually sensations in the mind. It is these images or sense data that we know by acquaintance. This is roughly Descartes's and Locke's "twofold existence" theory that we are only directly aware of ideas, but expressed in the terminology of sense data, acquaintance and description.

There are also other theories of perception. The basic problem of perception is the nature of sensation and its relation to the perception of physical objects. We sometimes misread sensations and sometimes have sensations without corresponding objects; that is, things may not be as they appear. The question is how we are to analyse propositions describing these appearings. The following is the basic form of an appearing statement:

(1) *O* appears *F* to *S*.

where *O* is a physical object, *F* a property and *S* a subject perceiving *O*. An example is 'The table appears rectangular' or 'The apple appears green'. There are three main theories of appearing statements: (i) the sense-datum theory; (ii) the appearing theory; and (iii) the adverbial theory.

(i) The sense-datum theory analyses appearing statements in terms of sense data, so that (1) is equivalent to (2):

(2) *S* directly apprehends a sense datum of *O* which is *F*.

According to this, if I perceive the table obliquely from the edge, I apprehend a sense datum that is trapezoidal. That is, 'The table appears trapezoidal to me' is analysed as 'I am directly apprehending a trapezoidal sense datum of the table'.

(ii) The appearing theory takes (1) to express an unanalysable relation between a perceiver, a physical object and a quality. When we look at the table from an angle, we are directly aware of it, not of an intervening object, but it looks or appears trapezoidal to us. The appearance lies in the way the object appears; it is not a sense datum that has the property that is appearing to us.

This has certain advantages over a sense-datum theory. It preserves the common-sense belief that we directly perceive physical objects and does not commit us to a "twofold existence" theory, which Berkeley and others find so offensive to common sense. But it also has difficulty explaining "wild" illusions in which no object appears at all. It works well for "mild" illusions such as when the table appears trapezoidal or a leaf on the road appears to be a frog, since we can identify existent objects in these cases that are appearing to us. But there are no existent objects in dreams, hallucinations or schizophrenic delusions (such as John Nash's delusions in the film *A Beautiful Mind*). In these cases, the theory is driven to holding that it is a brain state or an image that does the appearing. When Nash was imagining his roommate talking to him, some aberrant state of his brain was appearing to be talking to him. There are ways of making this more plausible, but this has led to a third theory.

(iii) The adverbial theory interprets sensations as *ways of appearing*. This analyses the appearing statement (1) as:

(3) S is being appeared to in an *F-like* manner.

The property is not treated as an adjective qualifying a sense datum, but adverbially as a way of appearing. This is clearer if we re-express (3) as 'S is being appeared to *F-ly*'. When we perceive the table, we are appeared to trapezoidally, and when we see the leaf that looks like a frog, we are appeared to in a frog-like manner or frog-ily. These adverbial constructions are awkward and grammatically unnatural, but they are necessary to express the theory's main claim, namely, that a sensation is not an awareness of a sense datum distinct from the object or of an actual object appearing in a certain way. The content of the sensation is just a mode of the basic mental act of sensing.

It is not necessary to decide between these theories. How to analyse sensations is on the borderline between epistemology and the philosophy of mind (which is part of metaphysics or perhaps psychology). The important epistemic issue is the nature of the *cognitive* relation of sensing. As they are usually presented, all three theories take sensing to be direct apprehension or Russell's acquaintance, that is, sensation is immediate non-propositional knowledge and so provides a stopping place for justifying empirical knowledge.

Russell's theory of acquaintance helps to clarify this, since he has more to say about sensations than proponents of the other theories. According to Russell, sense data are the direct objects of *sensations*, which are acts of awareness. He takes this terminology to be clearer than earlier theories, which talk of 'ideas' or 'appearances'. Consider the following propositions:

(1) S has a sensation of O.
(2) S is acquainted with a sense datum of O.
(3) S is acquainted with an idea of O.
(4) S is acquainted with an appearance of O.

Russell holds that (2) is the analysis of (1). Proposition (3) is the Lock-ean analysis of (1) where 'idea' is taken as the object of the awareness, not the awareness itself. Russell thinks (2) is preferable, since 'idea' implies that the object of a sensation is a mental entity, while 'sense datum' is neutral and leaves the datum's ontological status open. With (2), we can claim that sense data are mental or that they are real enti-ties; we can even hold that physical objects are composed of sense data without committing ourselves to Berkeleyan idealism. Proposition (4) is the analysis of sensation deriving from Kant. The problem with it is that 'appearance' implies that there is *something* of which it is an appearance and this is also a further question, according to Russell. If we use the appearance terminology, we prejudge the question raised by Berkeley's idealism, namely, whether physical objects just are sense data (and mental ones at that) and whether there are further somethings of which they are appearances.

It is clear from this that Russell wants to distinguish between the epistemic and metaphysical questions raised by sensations. The epis-temic point is that a sensation is a *form of knowledge* of an object, while the metaphysical status of this object is not strictly epistemological. He holds that this mode of knowing is direct and exists independently of any other knowledge or inference. We may say that objects known in this way are *given* to the mind, while things of which we are indirectly aware are based on inference.

Another important feature of acquaintance for Russell is that the object must exist in order for us to be aware of it. I may be mistaken about the table now because I may be dreaming, but I cannot be mistaken about my being directly aware of table-like sense data. Whether I am dreaming or hallucinating, I am certain of my sensations and the existence of my sense data. Finally, Russell does not restrict acquaintance to awareness of sense data, but thinks we are also acquainted with universals and relations.

To summarize, Russell holds that (a) sensations are acts of acquaintance with sense data, and that to be acquainted with an object (b) our awareness must not rest on any inference or other knowledge, and finally (c) the object of acquaintance must be real.

Russell's foundationalism is based on this theory. He holds that perceptual judgements are known on the basis of acquaintance with sense data. I know that there is a table in front of me because (i) I am acquainted with a brown trapezoidal datum and, on the basis of this, directly know (ii) that this sense datum is brown and trapezoidal. And, by appealing to this, memory beliefs and background generalizations, I infer (iii) that there is a table here. The foundation is not acts of acquaintance but beliefs about sense data such as (ii). When I am acquainted with a datum, I can read off its properties by inspection (without inference). These propositions are known by intuition and are the *basic premises* on which all empirical knowledge is based. We might say that the foundation lies in sensations, but Russell prefers to say that it lies in the premises we read off them, since the foundation is the stopping place in giving reasons, and must be expressed in propositions. Even though Russell is not an empiricist, this may be seen as a clarification of Locke's and Hume's theory of the foundation of empirical knowledge.

The myth of the given

The main problem with all three accounts (the sense-datum theory, the appearing theory and the adverbial theory) is their claim that the awareness of data or ideas is independent of inference and other knowledge, or that they are *given* to the mind. In this section, we will consider the charge by Sellars that this theory is a myth and, in the next, his criticism of an alternative foundations theory based on reliability and his defence of a coherence theory.

Sellars holds that in order to be *given* mental states must be *non-inferential* and *presuppositionless* (Sellars 1963: §VIII ¶32). Non-inferential states are not the result of *conscious* reasoning, but occur spontaneously. Presuppositionless states do not presuppose prior beliefs, knowledge or learning. He agrees that sensations are non-inferential in this sense, but denies that this shows that they are not based on subconscious inferential processes. The theory of the given accepts the following argument:

(1) We have an innate capacity to be aware of sorts, for example, things that are red or triangular.
(2) This capacity is triggered by experience, but not shaped by it.
Thus (3) This awareness does not depend on subconscious processing and so is presuppositionless.

Premise (1) claims that we have innate dispositions to recognize qualities and (2) that these dispositions do not have to be moulded by experience. The only role experience plays is to present the opportunity for recognition to occur. Sellars accepts (1) but rejects (2). We have innate cognitive dispositions, but they must be structured by experience and education in order to be activated.

This controversy is similar to the one over innatism. Descartes's innate ideas are abstract ideas such as perfection and infinity, or ideas of unobservable entities such as God. He denies that these are acquired by abstraction from sense experience or introspection and so are innate. The theory of the given holds that we have an innate faculty to recognize physical objects and our mental states that is triggered by experience but not shaped by it. The issue in both cases is whether the mind has abilities that do not derive from nature and experience, but have to be implanted in us by extra-natural agency.

Price and Sellars on the given

… when I say that it is "directly" present to my consciousness, I mean that my consciousness of it is not reached by inference, nor by any other intellectual process (such as abstraction or intuitive induction), nor by any other intellectual process from sign to significate. There obviously must be some sort or sorts of presence to consciousness which can be called "direct" in this sense, else we should have an infinite regress.

(Price 1950: 3)

… there are various forms taken by the myth of the given in this connection, depending on other philosophical commitments. But they all have in common the idea that the awareness of certain *sorts* – and by "sorts" I have in mind, in the first instance, determinate sense repeatables – is a primordial, non-problematic feature of "immediate experience".

(Sellars 1963: ¶26)

Sellars has two arguments against innate cognitive abilities. The first is based on the distinction between sensations as physical stimuli and cognitive states. Our senses are often stimulated by physical objects without our being aware of them. When we look around the room, we have stimuli from all the objects in it even though we do not notice them all. Similarly, when we walk though the mall, we "see" people and displays that do not register in consciousness. We are constantly receiving information from the environment that fails to catch our attention, but most of these sensations are not cognitive. Sellars argues that a necessary condition for having sensations in the sense of awarenesses is that we have the appropriate concepts. A child who does not know what a clock is would not be aware of it, although it might be aware of a round something on the wall, if it had the concepts of wall and roundness.

According to Sellars, the doctrine of the given slides between these two senses of 'sensation'. We clearly have an innate ability to have *physical stimulations* from the environment, but it is not clear that we can recognize colours and shapes without previous learning and experience. In order to have *cognitive* sensations, we must have the appropriate concepts and there is no reason to think these are innate and unlearned. To have a (cognitive) sensation of an object O, S must be aware of O as having some quality, and this requires that he have concept of the quality.

This argument assumes (i) that awareness is always conceptual and (ii) that all concepts are acquired by experience. Defenders of the given usually deny (i). Russell's theory of acquaintance is a classic illustration of this. He thinks we can be aware of a red patch without having any prior experience and, further, that this is the way we acquire the concept of redness. The red datum is directly present and we notice that it is red; no prior learning or association is necessary. We can then judge that the external object is red. Sellars's view is based on the claim that all cognition rests on judgement. To be aware of something is to be aware of it as falling under a predicate or general concept. If this is right, we cannot be aware of a red patch without being aware of it as being red (or some other colour) and so cannot acquire the concept of red from the awareness.

One problem with this is that Sellars assumes that conceptual thought (including belief, recognition and awareness) depends on language, which implies that creatures without language cannot have beliefs or think. This might be the case, but we cannot simply assume that it is. Animals do not seem to be able to frame arguments or have abstract ideas, but they may still think. The minimal requirements for being a thinking being are (i) the ability to indicate or refer to objects and (ii) the ability to recognize similarities, that is, the ability to refer to discrete individuals and events and to classify them with other individuals. And some animals may have these abilities even though they lack language. (Consider, for instance, how the higher mammals respond to danger.) At least, we cannot rule this out *a priori*.

There is a better argument for Sellars's claim, however. The main evidence for the given is introspection: when we sense a red datum, it seems to be directly perceived in a way that does not presuppose other mental states. The experience we have when an apple appears red or the fire appears warm seems self-contained and the data directly present. This is true enough, but it only shows that the content of a sensation is not the result of *conscious* reasoning, which Sellars admits; it does not show that they are presuppositionless and do not result from subconscious suggestion and inference. In fact introspection is restricted to the present and cannot show anything about the ancestry of an awareness. All we know is their present status. Secondly, psychology shows that most concepts are based on associations in the early stages even though we are not aware of them. For instance, we have to learn to associate visual and tactual data in order to perceive three-dimensionally, as Berkeley argued. Our view of ourselves is that we are independent and autonomous observers of our experience, but this does not mean that awareness does not rest on prior experience.

John Stuart Mill (1806–1873) offered a similar argument in the nineteenth century. He distinguishes between the *introspective method* and the *psychological method* in psychology (*Examination*: ch. IX). The introspective method takes the basic data to be what we are conscious of as adults and avoids hypotheses about mental states; it takes introspective data at face value and builds from there. As an influential contemporary of his put it, "Consciousness is to the philosopher what the Bible is to the theologian" (Hamilton 1877: 52), that is, the study of the mind. His meaning was that we must take our mental life in the same way theology takes the Bible: without examining it critically. Mill thinks this is the wrong approach. The mind has to be studied as an extension of our lives as animals and examined critically by hypotheses in the same way physics explains observable data. This is the psychological method.

These matters aside, it is also not clear that introspection supports givenness. Appearing and sense-data statements are supposed to describe the given qualities of experience, their "look" and "feel", rather than how we interpret them in the light of prior associations. But there are also appearing statements that have a strong belief component. These are *doxastic* appearings and contrast with *phenomenal* appearings. Consider the following:

(1) The apple appears red.
(2) The dress appears expensive.
(3) Incest appeared acceptable to the Egyptians.
(4) The Yankees appear to be the team to beat.

The red look of the apple is a phenomenal aspect of it and seems directly present to us. But 'appear' does not have this meaning in the other sentences. In (2) it means that I am *inclined to believe* that it is expensive, in (3) that the Egyptians *believed* that incest was acceptable, and in (4) that the evidence points to the Yankees as the team to beat. Evidence for this is that they cannot be put into sense-datum terminology. While (1) can plausibly be expressed as 'The sense datum of the apple is red', it is nonsense to express (2) as 'The sense datum of the dress is expensive'. Sense data cannot be expensive; they can only have sensed qualities such as colour and shape. Similar comments apply to (3) and (4).

The theory of the given holds that only phenomenal appearings are given or directly present. Doxastic appearings presuppose prior experience, since the concepts of being expensive and the team to beat cannot be acquired by acquaintance. The same may be said of the concept of moral acceptability in (3). Only a limited range of qualities are given in sense experience, such as colour, taste, smell, size, shape and temperature. The others are doxastic interpretations and have to be learned.

The problem is that this distinction is not as sharp as the theory requires. The theory holds that a dress cannot literally look expensive since this presupposes other knowledge. But in fact an expensive dress can look expensive in the same way it looks white even though this is based on association. To hold that it cannot and is just a belief state misinterprets the experience.

A less controversial example is this. Experienced wine drinkers can often tell what region a wine is from by its taste. A Bordeaux wine can taste St Emilion-ly or Medoc-ly. To say that a wine tastes St Emilion-ly or Medoc-ly is not just a matter of belief, although beliefs may be based on them. The tastes are different even though we learn to recognize them by experience. Introspection fails to tell us that they are presuppositionless and we have to turn to Mill's psychological method to find out that they presuppose other experience. Similarly music by different composers often has a distinctive phenomenal sound. Mozart sounds different from Beethoven and Wagner even though it is not detectible to listeners with no experience of classical music.

The problem is that givenism holds that only a small range of qualities can be phenomenally present to us: colour, shape, taste, temperature, feel and smell. These are known by acquaintance and all other qualities are known by description. Only these are presuppositionless qualities of sense data. But this is not what introspection tells us. Associative qualities also appear to be presuppositionless when they obviously are not. This suggests that the theory is just another psychological hypothesis about the status of sense qualities and, without a sharp introspective distinction to support it, nothing more than a dogma – or a myth. The more likely story is that *all* qualities are based on learning and experience, as Sellars holds.

Reliability and Sellars's coherence theory

It is sometimes thought that rejecting the given implies a rejection of foundationalism. Although Sellars thinks this is ultimately right, he also suggests a way of defending the foundations theory without the given. This theory is usually called *reliabilism*. Let us look at his explanation of this, then at his coherence theory of justification.

Reliabilism and foundations

One of the problems facing a coherence theory is that it does not allow for a connection between beliefs and the world. If justification depends only on inferential relations between beliefs, the system seems unconnected with reality and cannot plausibly give knowledge of it.

Sellars has a reply to this. He holds that even if justification rests on coherence alone, there is still a causal relation between our beliefs and the world. If we have the necessary concepts and are able to recognize observable qualities, physical stimuli will cause us to have spontaneous beliefs under favourable conditions. These are interpretations based on associations but do not involve conscious reasoning. There is thus a psychological foundation for empirical knowledge. Observational premises are not assumptions or the result of agreement; they are forced on us. Further, although justifying them might lead to a regress or be circular, they are still a clear starting-point for further inferences.

Sellars says that normal adults have the ability to recognize colours and shapes, and even when dresses are expensive or the music is Mozart's. Their beliefs are reliable indicators of their surroundings. A minimal condition for someone's utterance 'This is green' to have epistemic authority is that some statement of the form *X is a reliable symptom of Y* is true of him, that is, he must be a reliable guide of the colours of things. This suggests the following epistemic principle:

> If *S* is a reliable judge of colours in standard conditions, his spontaneous beliefs about the colours of nearby objects are truth-conducive and have warrant.

There are several ways of putting this. A reliable perceiver is analogous to a reliable thermometer, or, more generally, a *reliable meter*. He gives us accurate information about the world just as a working thermometer tells us about the temperature. We can also say that he is a *source of evidence* about the world. For a cognitive being to be able to meter the environment, he must acquire a mechanism whose input is physical stimuli and output beliefs. If a significant proportion of these outputs are true, he is a reliable source of evidence about the world and his spontaneous beliefs can serve as premises for other beliefs.

Sellars calls this "the thermometer view" and rejects it, but it is also a reliabilist alternative to the theory of the given. The theory holds that beliefs that result from the stimulation of reliable perceptual mechanisms have some credibility and provide the epistemic input for the rest of our empirical beliefs.

This foundations theory has two advantages. First, it explains the sense in which we directly perceive physical objects. The stimulus on the sense organs starts a process that causes cognitive output in the form of a belief about the object. Since this is the first cognitive step in the process, we can give a clear sense to the claim that we immediately perceive physical objects. There are other steps in the process, but they fall on the non-cognitive physical side. Secondly, the theory does not over-intellectualize perception by making it seem that we are constantly reading reports from observations of sense data. A better description of perception is that we are unconscious processors of information, receiving data and producing mental states that are premises for inference and reasons for action. This makes human perception continuous with animal perception. Higher animals have no language but they may still have perceptual beliefs that influence their behaviour. The result is a naturalistic conception of perception.

Sellars's defence of the coherence theory

Although he is a founder of reliabilism, Sellars does not accept it. He thinks human beings are not mere meters and uses the term 'thermometer view' derisively. To have beliefs and evidence, one must be more than a meter of the environment; one must also be able to make inferences, have concepts and decide between competing beliefs – abilities he thinks can only be acquired by learning a language, that is, by learning to make what he calls word–word connections in addition to word–world connections. Furthermore, one must be able to reflect on one's abilities and evaluate them. This leads him beyond a foundations theory to a coherence theory.

The thermometer theory (i.e. reliabilism) we have been considering holds two theses:

(i) Perception is non-inferential, but not self-authenticating or presuppositionless.
(ii) Being reliable is sufficient to give perceptual beliefs epistemic authority.

The first is a rejection of the given and the second makes perceptual beliefs the ultimate basis of empirical knowledge. Sellars argues that (ii) is false. The authority of perception cannot derive solely from our being reliable perceivers. We must also be aware that we are, that is, be able to reflect on our abilities and *show* that they are reliable. To do this we must have a picture of ourselves and our relation to the environment, and this implies that the ultimate basis of knowledge is coherence.

His reason is that we can evaluate a perceptual ability only by appealing to perception. The standard procedure would be to keep track of one's judgements, then compare them with reality. But, if empiricism is right, the only way to get information about reality is by perception. This means that we can evaluate a perceptual mechanism only by assuming perception is reliable. To be a reliable judge of facts of kind K, all or most of our perceptual judgements about K-type facts must be true; but we can only know this by perception. Hence we can evaluate the ability only by assuming it, which is circular. Sellars thinks this commits us to a coherence theory. We have justified beliefs only when we have a large number of beliefs and see that they form a coherent system. Before this we are thermometers. Others may use us as a reliable source of information about the world if they know we are reliable, but our beliefs are not justified until we realize this ourselves. When the beliefs cohere, they all acquire positive epistemic status together.

Sellars's work has had a wide influence. First, his criticism of the given led to the virtual disappearance of traditional foundations theories such as Russell's and spawned a number of *reliabilist* theories. Secondly, his positive theory revived interest in coherence theories that Russell and his contemporaries had rejected at the start of the twentieth century. Thirdly, it turned epistemology from the study of sense data and the nature of sensation to questions about sources of evidence and the nature of reliability. We cannot discuss the intricacies of these debates here, but a discussion of the basic issue between the foundation and coherence theories might serve as an introduction.

Foundations and coherence

Let us try to state the difference between foundations and coherence theories more precisely. Foundationalism is sometimes taken to require that the basic premises of knowledge must be absolutely certain or unrevisable, but this is too strong. Its main claim is that coherence alone does not justify beliefs; some beliefs must have warrant that derives from experience, not from other propositions. The parts of a novel may hang together perfectly, but the result is still a fiction and tells us nothing about the world, while a work of history weaves a story based on facts established independently. Another misconception is that a foundations theory has no role for coherence in empirical knowledge; propositions are justified solely by their relation to the basic propositions. More sophisticated versions hold that knowledge is a system of beliefs justified by basic premises *and* their internal relations.

This suggests that a minimal foundations theory holds that some beliefs have warrant because of their relation to experience independent of their relations to other beliefs. Traditionally the basic premises have been taken to be appearing (or sense-datum) statements from which perceptual propositions about physical objects such as 'There is the car' or 'I see John by the tree' are derived, but for simplicity we may take physical-object statements to be basic. One theory holds that a perceptual belief is justified if we have an appropriate experience. Suppose I hear what I take to be the school bus on the street outside. I would be justified if it were Saturday and I know that there is no school at the weekend or if I were unable to distinguish between the sounds of a bus and a delivery truck. The justification is *prima facie* in that it may be overridden by counter-evidence or if I cannot make fine enough discriminations in the experiences. The main point from the standpoint of foundationalism is that my ability to interpret experience in the absence of overriding or defeating evidence is *sufficient* for the belief to be justified; I do not also have to have evidence that I am reliable, as Sellars argues. An even weaker foundations theory hold that being a reliable interpreter of experience does not produce justified beliefs, but only provides *some* warrant, which must be supplemented by coherence with other beliefs to make it fully justified. Both theories are foundationalist, since they deny that coherence alone can provide evidence; some beliefs must have warrant deriving from experience itself.

In light of this, we may say that a minimal foundations theory holds that some beliefs have initial credibility or warrant independent of their relations with other propositions, while a coherence denies this and claims that coherence alone is sufficient to explain evidence. We can also distinguish two broad classes of foundations theories: those that base initial credibility on some facts being given to us and theories that base it on reliable perceptual mechanisms. Let us put aside theories resting on the given and concentrate on reliabilist and coherentist theories (see key point "A classification of theories").

These theories offer different pictures of empirical knowledge. The foundationalist holds that it is a structure resting on a base of propositions that acquire epistemic authority from the knower's ability to meter the environment, while the coherentist holds that it is a system of propositions that support one another so that its members acquire warrant as a group and not individually. It is sometimes said that the foundationalist recognizes only *linear* lines of justification traceable to the basic premises, which provided epistemic input, while the coherentist takes justification to be *holistic* and to proceed by something akin to quantum jumps: at one time, no member of the set has warrant and at a later time, each member does.

The main difficulty with the coherence theory is this notion of holist justification. If no beliefs have warrant individually, how does a set of them acquire it all at once? The theory says that it does, but how it does so is left mysterious. It is analogous to saying that if you collect enough empty boxes of sweets, you will suddenly have some sweets in each of them. Talk of holistic justification is just hand-waving. The foundations theory, on the other hand, can explain linear justification. It holds that when you become a reliable reader of certain kinds of facts, your spontaneous beliefs about them become initially credible. Some state of the world stimulates the sense organs and a belief is formed because you have the ability to interpret facts of this kind. Hence there is some likelihood that the belief is true and the belief has warrant it can pass on to other beliefs. Despite its vagueness, this story offers an intelligible account of how we get epistemic input from the world while coherentism's non-linear justification does not.

As we noted, the foundations theory still assigns an important role to coherence. Once we have a set of credible beliefs, coherence takes over and moves some of them to a higher level. Suppose, for instance, that my success rate in spotting robins in good light in middle distance is 0.3. This is very low reliability, since it means that a belief that there is a robin on the lawn at any moment has less than an even chance of being true. But if I look over a period of five seconds and judge four times that it is a robin, the chance that one of these judgements is true increases to about 0.75, and if I look twice more, this increases to 0.87. (The calculation is this: the chance that one belief is false is $1 - 0.3 = 0.7$. The chance that all four beliefs are false is $0.7 \times 0.7 \times 0.7 \times 0.7$ or about 0.25. Hence the chance that at least one of them is true is about 0.75.) Even though the likelihood that any one belief is true is small, continuous processing of information quickly produces beliefs that are highly likely. And from here coherence and inferential relations between beliefs can take over and produce beliefs with higher levels of credibility.

Secondly, this theory is consistent with holding that justification at higher levels depends on other (justified) beliefs and our ability to offer arguments. It is a *perceptual reliability theory*, and does not commit us to more usual versions of reliabilism, which hold that all justification is based on reliable mechanisms, no matter how far removed the beliefs are from the foundation. These reliability theories may be defensible, but it is never made clear how one might be justified in accepting a theoretical belief such as the big-bang theory of physics by a reliable mechanism. But these issues lie beyond the controversy between foundationalism and coherence theories of justification.

The main problem facing reliabilism is that the epistemic status of perceptual beliefs depends on a condition external to the believer. He may have credible beliefs without being aware of it since whether he does or not depends on whether he is a reliable meter and not on whether he is aware of this. Nor can he check perception to verify his reliability since the only way of telling that a previous belief is true is by looking again. This is not a problem if we assume other cognitive abilities. A person learning to identify birds can learn that he is acquiring the skill by using a bird guide with pictures and descriptions. In this case, he is learning a specialized perceptual skill against the background of other perceptual skills. (Children learn to perceive in this way by being corrected by their parents and experimenting on their own.) But this will not work at the global level. We cannot learn that we are reliable meters of the environment by perception when the question is the reliability of perception itself. The result is that the reliability of perception is an external condition we cannot justify non-circularly. This is analogous to Hume's problem of induction and a similar problem arises for memory. This means that empirical knowledge rests on assumptions of reliability we cannot discharge non-circularly. Even though we may have a foundation for empirical beliefs about particulars, the epistemic principles themselves cannot be justified and we are back with the skeptic's regress argument. A useful name for theories that hold that knowledge may be actual even though it rests on conditions the knower cannot justify is *externalism*, while *internalism* holds that you are not justified unless you have some reason for believing the conditions obtain. We shall return to this in Chapter 6.

This reliance on undischarged conditions may have been what Sellars had in mind when he called the appeal to reliability without a background justification a thermometer theory. It reduces knowers to meters who can monitor facts in the world but cannot learn that they are succeeding. If this is the end of the matter, knowledge is a shadow of what we think it is, since it is relative to conditions we cannot show obtain. No matter how careful we are, we might be in the same position as Russell's chicken, which relies on induction in trusting the farmer and ends up on the dining room table (Russell 1959: ch. 6).

Some critics have found this intolerable and have sought refuge in coherentism. BonJour argues that this externalist reliabilism violates one

---

KEY POINT *A classification of theories*

Foundationalism

| Coherentism | Givenism | Reliabilism |

Internalism Externalism

- *Foundationalism*: some beliefs have credibility independent of all others.
- *Coherentism*: No beliefs have such credibility.
- *Externalism*: Knowledge rests on assumptions we cannot justify.
- *Internalism*: Knowledge cannot rest on such assumptions.

Coherentism and foundationalism exclude one another, but foundationalism includes givenism and reliabilism.
Internalism and externalism exclude one another, but both coherentism and givenism are versions of internalism, while reliabilism is an externalist theory.

---

of the traditional requirements of justified belief (BonJour 2000: 267). Philosophers have held that justification must be (i) truth-conducive and (ii) defensible. Reliabilism recognizes (i), but breaks with tradition on (ii). Unfortunately, this is not a persuasive argument against reliabilism, since the reliabilist thinks there are positive reasons for going against tradition. The objection also misrepresents the traditional view of justification. In addition to (i) and (ii), the traditional notion requires that it be (iii) non-circular. The reliabilist foundations theory opts for (i) and (iii) and rejects (ii), while coherentism accepts (i) and (ii) and rejects (iii). As a result, the appeal to tradition is inconclusive. We cannot pursue this debate here, but we shall have more to say about the requirement of defensibility in Chapter 6.

Summary

In this chapter, we have discussed:

- the skeptic's argument that the justification of beliefs must rest on a foundation, be circular, lead to a regress or rest on premises taken as assumptions;
- the theory of the given and its relation to Russell's knowledge acquaintance and Sellars's charge that givenness is a myth;
- the merits of perceptual reliabilism as an alternative;
- the controversy over foundationalism and coherentism, and their relations to the question of externalism versus internalism.

five

Empiricism and the *a priori*

The *a priori* poses special problems for empiricism. Mathematics and logic are the best examples we have of knowledge, the most certain and the most precise, yet they do not seem to be based on experience. Propositions such as '5 + 2 = 7' and 'Nothing can be true and false at the same time' also appear to be necessary and are true no matter what our experiences are. How can such truths be based on experience? Curiously enough, the *a priori* also poses a problem for rationalism, since there is no clear account of what it is to be known independently of experience. This chapter will explain some of the approaches empiricists have taken to the problem and why they have been led to skepticism about the very existence of *a priori* knowledge. But first we must become clearer about the basic distinctions on which the debate is based.

Necessity, the analytic and the *a priori*

Necessity and contingency

Necessary truths are propositions whose negations imply a contradiction. That '5 + 2 = 7' is such a proposition. To hold that it does not equal seven, but six or eight instead is contradictory. Similarly 'Whatever is, is' cannot be denied without contradiction. If John went to the store, he went to the store. We cannot claim that he did and did not go in the same sense, since this is contradictory. It is sometimes argued that he can go to the store and not go, since he can go to the store and the tanning salon. But this is not a contradiction. 'John went to the market' does not claim that he went *only* to the market. It leaves open that he made other stops as well. It also does not imply that he did not go to the salon.

Other counter-examples have been offered. It is sometimes said that there are exceptions to the principle of non-contradiction. Mary may be tall with respect to her classmates, but not with respect to the other members of the basketball team, and so she can be both tall and not tall at the same time. But this is not what the law of non-contradiction claims. As Aristotle pointed out, it holds that the same thing cannot both have a quality and not have it *at the same time* and *in the same respect*. Mary may be tall with respect to one standard and not to another, but no one can be tall and not tall with respect to the same standard.

Another explication of necessity is that a necessary truth is true in every possible or conceivable world. If John tells his mother that he will either be home by midnight or not, he has not given her any information. No matter what time he gets home, he will either be home by 12 or not, since it is a necessary truth that every proposition is either true or not true, that is, *Either p or not-p* is necessary, since it is true for any world you can think of. She wants to know what time he will get home *in this world*. To give an answer that holds no matter what happens tells her nothing.

It is for reasons like this that Leibniz held that necessary truths tell us about the structure of any possible world; they are true no matter what world exists or, as Leibniz would have put it, no matter what world God created. He distinguished three types of proposition:

- *Necessary truths*: propositions true in every possible or conceivable world.
- *Contradictions*: propositions false in every possible or conceivable world.
- *Contingent propositions*: propositions true in some world and false in other possible worlds.

Leibniz called the last kind *contingent* propositions since they are contingent on God's choice of which world to create, that is, their truth-value depends on which of the possible worlds is the actual one.

Logical principles are a special class of necessary truths. Montaigne tells the story of a duke who gave a dinner in honour of a bishop. Before the bishop arrived, the duke boasted of how well he knew him. He said that he was the bishop's first penitent. Later the bishop told the gathering of his long and varied career, and said that his first penitent as a young

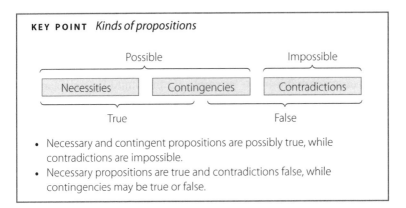

KEY POINT *Kinds of propositions*

Possible		Impossible
Necessities	Contingencies	Contradictions
True		False

- Necessary and contingent propositions are possibly true, while contradictions are impossible.
- Necessary propositions are true and contradictions false, while contingencies may be true or false.

priest confessed that he had murdered someone. If the duke and bishop were both right, it follows that the duke was a murderer. The reason is that (1) the duke was the first penitent and (2) the first penitent was a murderer together imply that (3) the duke was a murderer. The principle governing this inference is also a necessary truth and may be expressed as: *If A is B and B is C, then A is C,* whose negation is a contradiction. This means that if you want to reject the consequent that *A* is *C,* you must deny that *A* is *B* or that *B* is *C* (or both).

Analytic and synthetic

The distinction between necessary and contingent truths corresponds to Hume's distinction between relations of ideas and matters of fact. As we saw, Hume holds that relations of ideas can be known on the basis of the concepts alone, while matters of fact always require experience. This brings in another distinction to which we have already alluded: the distinction between analytic and synthetic propositions. An *analytic* proposition, according to Kant, is one whose subject term contains its predicate term. An example is 'All mothers are female'. Anyone who knows what a mother is knows that the concept of mother contains that of being female. Other examples are 'A triangle is a three-sided figure' and 'Logic studies arguments'. 'No mothers are male' is also analytic, since being male excludes being female. If we know what 'mother' and 'male' mean, we know that this is true. *Synthetic* propositions go beyond the meanings of the terms and so are not trivially true. 'All mothers love their children' is an example. This may be true, but we cannot tell by the meanings of the terms alone. Nothing about the concept of mother implies that they love their children. Even if they all do, we cannot be sure that the next mother we meet will love her children, as we can be sure that she will be female.

Kant argues that there are also synthetic mathematical propositions. 'The internal angles of a triangle equal two right angles' and '5 + 2 = 7', he claims, are synthetic. His reason is that knowing the meanings of their subject terms is not sufficient to establish their truth. One can know what a triangle is and that two right angles equal 180 degrees without knowing that this is a property of triangles. Similarly one can know what '5', '2', '+' and '=' mean and not know that five and two equals seven. According to Kant, we need a special act of mind in order to know this, an act that synthesizes the elements of the subject term and sees that they equal seven. And in the case of the first proposition, we need to prove that the angles of a triangle equal 180 degrees by appealing to other geometric truths.

One problem with Kant's explanation of analyticity is that it applies only to subject–predicate propositions and not to logical truths. If analytic propositions are identified with what Locke called trifling propositions and do not convey information,

(1) John is either a baker or not a baker.

would seem to be analytic even though it is not a subject–predicate proposition and does not meet Kant's criterion. One way to deal with this is to revise the notion of analytic sentences as Frege did in the nineteenth century. On his account, a proposition is analytic if and only if (i) it is a logical truth or (ii) it can be turned into one by substituting synonymous terms for some of its general terms. On this criterion, (1) is analytic since it has the form *Either p or not-p*, which is a logical truth. And using both criteria, we can turn 'All mothers are female' into a logical truth. Since a mother is a female parent by definition, this is equivalent to 'All female parents are female' which has the form 'Everything that is both F and P is F', which is a logical truth.

On both Kant's and Frege's accounts, 'A triangle is a three-sided figure' is analytic and 'The internal angles of a triangle equal 180 degrees' is synthetic. The second is synthetic on Frege's theory because the concepts of a triangle or of its angles (or of both together) do not show that they add up to 180 degrees. As a result, the first would be said to be trifling or non-informative, and the second informative. But Frege's account makes '5 + 2 = 7' analytic while Kant's does not. Suppose we define '7' as 6 + 1, '6' as 5 + 1 and '2' as 1 + 1. From 7 = 7, which is true by identity, we can then derive 6 + 1 = 7, and from this 5 + 1 + 1 = 7, and finally 5 + 2 = 7.

The a priori

The concepts of necessity, possibility and impossibility are modal notions and are metaphysical concepts (since they describe kinds of truths), while the concept of analyticity is semantic (since it rests on the notion of meaning). The concept of *a priori* is epistemological. In its primary sense, it does not apply to propositions at all, but to how they are justified or known. Presumably God knows every true proposition *a priori* regardless of its modal or semantic status, that is, he knows it to be true by thought alone without appeal to experience. By extension we can say that a proposition is *a priori* if it can be justified *a priori* by a finite knower. But this still takes the basic notion to be epistemic and does not explain it in non-epistemic terms. Furthermore, it does not tell us what the *a priori* is in itself, but only explains it negatively as justification that is *not* empirical. We know what it is to know something by sense experience and something known *a priori* is described as known (or justified) but not by sense experience. The only positive accounts rely on metaphors usually related to perception. Russell says, for example, that *a priori* knowledge is *seen* to be true, is known by *insight* or is *grasped*. If the proposition is self-evident, we have a direct *insight* that it is true, and if it is not self-evident, we know it by self-evident steps from self-evident axioms. Self-evidence is usually characterized as direct seeing or grasping of truth or, as Locke put it, a proposition is self-evident if and only if we immediately perceive that it is true once we understand it. And since all these metaphors derive from sense perception, they do not get us very far. We shall return to this below in § "The notion of the *a priori*" (p. 109).

The problem posed by the *a priori* for empiricism can be put as follows. The empiricist holds that no knowledge of real existence is *a priori*. The rationalist offers this argument:

> (1) Mathematical and logical knowledge is *a priori*.
> (2) It informs us of real existence.
> Thus (3) There is *a priori* knowledge of real existence, i.e. empiricism is false.

In order to reject this conclusion, the empiricist must reject one of the premises. Locke accepts (1) but rejects (2) and is followed in this by Berkeley and Hume. This is also the position of the logical positivists in the twentieth century. The more radical approach is to reject the claim that mathematics is *a priori*. This is the view of John Stuart Mill, and the American logicians and pragmatists C. S. Peirce and W. V. Quine.

Let us look more closely at the views of Locke, Mill and Quine, then turn to the concept of the *a priori* and some criticisms of it, especially by Peirce.

Varieties of empiricism

Locke's nominalist response

We have already alluded to Locke's account of the *a priori*. He holds that arithmetic and geometry are *a priori* (although he eschews this word), but claims that they are based on definitions, and these in turn are based on convention. There is no independent realm of mathematical entities of which they are true.

The standard interpretation is that Locke holds that mathematical truths are analytic and trifling, but this is not his view. He believes that outright definitions such as 'A triangle is a three-sided figure' are trifling, but that 'A triangle's internal angles equal two right angles' is informative. This is also Hume's view. Using Kant's terminology, they hold that mathematical propositions may be either analytic or synthetic *a priori*. Many critics have found this confused. Following Kant, they hold that informative mathematical truths must depict an independent realm of necessary truths and cannot be purely nominal. This is anachronistic, however. Locke was not working in the Kantian tradition but a late medieval one. For Kant affirmative analytic propositions such as the definition of 'triangle' are true because the meaning of the predicate is included in the meaning of the subject. Locke's view seems to be that this is true of trifling propositions, but that informative mathematical propositions are based on the meanings of *all* the terms and not just those present in the proposition. We know the truth of 'The internal angles of a triangle equal two right angles' by reflecting on the meanings of each of the terms in conjunction with other geometric propositions and their meanings. This reflection produces new knowledge and is not trifling, but it is still based on the meanings of the terms and our conventions. To use medieval terminology, the proposition is known *ex vi terminorum*, that is, by way of the terms, and does not describe an independent realm of mathematical objects. This may be taken as an expanded conception of analyticity resembling Frege's, although it is not put as precisely.

Locke's main claim is that mathematical objects are fictions. He holds that only concrete particulars are real. Objects such as triangularity and the numbers are abstractions and so are human inventions. Berkeley puts the point this way:

In arithmetic therefore we regard not the *things* but the *signs*, which nevertheless are not regarded for their own sake, but because they direct us how to act with relation to things, and dispose rightly of them. ... [T]hose things which pass for abstract truths and theorems concerning numbers, are, in reality, conversant about no object distinct from particular numerable things, except only names and characters; which originally came to be considered, on no other account but their being *signs*, or capable to represent conveniently whatever particular things men had need to compute.   (*PHK*: §122)

This is a nominalist account of abstract entities and contrasts sharply with the realist view of Plato that they (and moral qualities such as justice and the good) exist independently of thought and particulars, a view openly advocated by Russell (see the Introduction above) and less obviously by Frege. The difference between Locke and the realists on this issue is metaphysical and not strictly epistemological. Both sides accept *a priori* knowledge and differ on whether it is about real objects. Locke is an empiricist because he rejects the Platonic account of the nature of mathematical truths, not because he denies that they are *a priori*.

It is sometimes said that empiricists are motivated by a distaste for an extreme metaphysical view. There may be some truth in this, but it should not obscure the fact that their main motivation is to reject any knowledge of reality that is not based on experience. As we saw in Chapter 1, Locke is willing to hold that the laws of nature governing real essences, that is, the configurations of the insensible corpuscles, are necessary truths and that we could know them as we know the laws of geometry if we had microscope-like eyes. Most empiricists agree with Hume that laws are contingent truths and cannot be necessary. Locke, however, finds the major difficulty in rationalism to lie in its claim to a super-sensible mode of knowledge of reality, not its postulation of necessary truths. With more powerful eyes, we might know the necessary principles by which physical objects interact. The point here is that this view shows that empiricism in general is consistent with real necessities in nature. We can accept them and remain empiricists, so long as we reject non-empirical knowledge of them.

This raises a point that is often overlooked in discussions of empiricism and mathematical knowledge. The exact nature of mathematical truths and how to explain them are issues for the philosophy of mathematics, not the theory of knowledge. The epistemological issue is how we come to know them. Philosophers of mathematics often discuss this issue, but usually they deal with non-epistemic questions such as how to analyse statements of arithmetic and geometry, and the relation between these and logical principles. Answers to these questions may or may not have implications for the theory of knowledge. If you lean towards an empiricist theory of knowledge and hold that they are about real entities, you *must* deny that our knowledge of them is *a priori*. Like metaphysics, the philosophy of mathematics is of interest in itself, but it is not a department of the theory of knowledge.

Mill's inductivist theory

The empiricism of Mill is more radical than Locke's (*System*: III xxiv 5, 6). He accepts the following theses:

- Mathematical propositions are not analytic or trifling, but are about real entities.
- The basic principles of mathematics, for example, the axioms of geometry and elementary arithmetic truths, are not *a priori* but are known on the basis of induction.
- Mathematical propositions are necessary, but Mill does not mean this in the ordinary sense; in his sense, necessity is consistent with contingency.

Let us look at these in more detail.

Mill's terms for 'analytic' and 'synthetic' are 'verbal' and 'real'. He says that arithmetic and geometric propositions are *real propositions*. By this he means that they are not analytic or trifling propositions, as Kant and Locke called them. Arithmetic is about numbers and these, he says, are always numbers of something. As a result, $2 + 1 = 3$ is not true by definition, but is about things in the world. We fail to see this because the proposition is abstract and does not mention a subject matter. It is not about cows or pebbles, but about aggregates of real things. Similarly, Mill holds that geometry is about angles and lines in nature. Furthermore they are known by induction based on our experiencing collections of things and observing the properties of lines, triangles and circles. Mathematics is thus an empirical science, differing from the other empirical sciences only in dealing with more abstract properties of particulars and their arrangements.

Mill sometimes writes as if each of us develops arithmetic and geometry out of our own experience, beginning with our play with objects in our cribs, but he is not committed to this. His view is that we learn mathematics from our parents and teachers, and accept it in the early stages on their authority, but that ultimately it is based on empirical evidence gathered long ago by early surveyors and merchants, and easily confirmed now. The natural sciences start with crude inductions that are corrected by further observation and inference and, Mill holds, the same is true of arithmetic and geometry. In their later stages physics and astronomy seem to be deductive sciences organized into levels of universal laws that are so familiar and obvious that they appear to be *a priori*, but they are still inductive. So is mathematics; familiarity makes it look conceptual and *a priori*, not a special kind of insight. The only source of evidence in any of the sciences is empirical and justification independent of this is an illusion.

Reading Mill in this way also allows him to avoid a charge that was often made against him by his contemporaries. They argued that he denies that the deductive sciences are genuine sciences, since he reduces scientific principles to disconnected truths that are neither certain nor precise. But Mill holds that being inductive does not preclude organizing a body of knowledge into a theory with axioms and theorems by means of deduction. He can also answer the charge that, even if elementary arithmetic truths – for example, $2 + 1 = 3$ – can be accepted as inductions, it is not plausible to hold that more complicated sums such as $21 + 33 = 54$ are also inductive. Since these are deduced from more elementary inductive truths (such as $3 + 1 = 4$ and $3 + 2 = 5$), they are also inductive.

This explains a famous objection made by Frege. He wonders what the observed or physical fact can be that is "asserted in the definition of the number 777864" and takes Mill to be committed to the absurd claim that every truth of arithmetic is known by generalization from instances (Frege 1960: 9). But this is not his view. Truths about 777864 are deduced from simpler propositions that, Mill holds, are known directly by induction. All arithmetic thus rests on an empirical base and can be taken to be about general features of physical reality.

Another objection Frege makes is that Mill "confuses the applications that can be made of an arithmetical proposition, which often are physical and do presuppose physical facts, with the pure mathematical proposition itself" (*Ibid.*: 13). Mill bases his case on examples such as *If we put two volumes of a liquid with five, we get seven volumes*, which, Frege says, are not part of the meaning of '$2 + 5 = 7$' but applications of it. This is right, but it is not clear that Mill confuses the meanings of arithmetic statements and their application. Logic holds that physical facts (and sensations) are what he calls *the ground* on the basis of which we ascribe attributes to objects, but he denies that this commits the logician to identifying the facts with the attributes. He may identify them or take them to have an independent existence, but these are questions of metaphysics and fall outside logic. Similarly, when we say that two volumes of liquid, when added together, will make seven volumes, we are not confusing the physical statement with the arithmetical statement that $2 + 5 = 7$, but citing grounds for it. Statements about physical aggregates (which are justified inductively) justify abstract arithmetical propositions, which in turn can be applied to further claims about physical objects (see *System*: I iii 9, 41–2; I v 7, 69).

A more problematic feature of Mill's theory is his defence of the necessity of mathematical propositions. He denies that they are necessary in the standard sense, that is, the sense in which p is a necessary truth if and only if its negation is a contradiction. They are necessary in that they follow necessarily from more basic mathematical truths. Let us look at this more closely.

When we deduce a proposition from premises, we may say that it is necessary even though it is a contingent truth. For example, we can say that it is necessary that Socrates is mortal, because he is human and all human beings are mortal. But 'Socrates is mortal' is not a necessary truth as it stands; in saying it is necessary, we only mean that it follows validly from other beliefs. This is *conditional necessity* as opposed to *absolute necessity*. A proposition is necessary in the absolute sense if its negation is a contradiction, and conditionally necessary if it necessarily follows in this sense from other truths. Unfortunately Mill's view only obscures the issue. Just as the critics argue, he holds that necessity in the standard sense is an illusion brought about by the fact that, when we accept certain premises, we are compelled to accept certain conclusions. We mistake this inferential and psychological compulsion for metaphysical necessity. But he continues to talk about mathematics as necessary. It would have been clearer if he had simply denied that there are any metaphysical necessities.

Another problem with Mill's theory is his claim that logic is inductive. He thinks that the law of non-contradiction is a generalization from experience. When we learn what 'is red' means, we learn by experience that nothing can be red and not red all over at the same time. We also learn that everything is either red or not red, which when generalized and corrected by other observations becomes the law of excluded middle. And the main principle of deductive inference is also inductive. This is the principle of the syllogism that Mill expresses as the law that "every mark of a mark is a mark of the object", that is, the principle that if x is F and F is G, x is also G. The syllogism about Socrates is an instance of this. From (1) Socrates is a human being and (2) every human being is a mortal, we may validly infer that (3) Socrates is mortal.

This creates two problems for Mill. First, he cannot defend his claim that geometry and arithmetic develop from isolated generalizations into sciences by deduction when deductive science itself is inductive. How can logic develop into a systematic body of knowledge when the principles that govern its development are principles of logic? Logic must have an independent basis in order to control induction in the other sciences. Secondly, syllogistic is not a powerful enough logic to serve as the handmaiden for mathematics and the other sciences. The main use of the syllogism is to extend knowledge by providing rules for subsumption of instances under universal propositions. It does not explain more complicated inferences.

The more serious of these problems is the first. The second makes his theory implausible, but he cannot be blamed for not having a more powerful logic than syllogistic. It was the only logic available to him and he had no way of knowing that a more powerful logic was in the incubation stage when he wrote. His *System of Logic* was published in 1843, four years before George Boole applied algebra to logic and initiated modern logic. The first problem, however, is fatal to his theory. As Aristotle recognized, logic is a theory of the rules of cogent thinking implicit in our thinking about the world, or, as it is sometimes said, logic is the critique of cogency. It is thus a second-order discipline about the rules for correct thinking in first-order disciplines. Like the theory of knowledge, it sets the standards for acceptable arguments and is not directly about the world. Indeed, this seems to be the motivation for holding that it is *a priori*. Since all thinking, inductive or deductive, presupposes it, it appears that it cannot be empirical, but must be *a priori*, or, if we reject this, have some other basis than induction.

Peirce and Quine

Writing a generation after Mill, Peirce disagreed with Mill on this point. He held that logical principles are implicit in reasoning about the world, but are not *a priori*. He distinguished three basic modes of inference: deduction, induction and hypothesis or abduction (Peirce 1955: ch. 11). Induction is generalizing from particulars and has the form *This is A, this is B, therefore All As are B*. Deduction has the form *All A is B, this is A, therefore this is B*, and hypothesis *All A is B, this is B, therefore this is*

A. Induction offers evidence for universal and statistical generalizations and, according to Peirce, is the basic source of all evidence. Deduction elaborates knowledge and enables us to systematize it, while abduction offers explanations.

Like induction, hypothetical inferences are formally invalid and may fail to produce true conclusions from true premises. This is clear if we consider an example. Consider the following arguments:

- *Induction*: Socrates is a Greek and loves Homer. Therefore, all Greeks love Homer.
- *Deduction*: All Greeks love Homer. Socrates is a Greek. Therefore, Socrates loves Homer.
- *Abduction*: All Greeks love Homer. Socrates loves Homer. Therefore, Socrates is a Greek.

The first argument is clearly invalid. A single instance of a Greek who loves Homer does not show that all of them do; and even if we sample a large number of Greeks, there is no guarantee that they all love Homer. Nevertheless, if a proportion of Greeks chosen at random love him, we may conclude provisionally that roughly the same proportion of unexamined Greeks also love him. The second is valid. Anyone who accepts the premises is compelled to accept the conclusion. The third, however, is not. The conclusion is true, but the premises do not prove that Socrates is Greek, for many non-Greeks also love Homer.

Peirce holds that logical theories are hypotheses offered to explain the rules for judging valid arguments of a certain class, for example, arguments resting on subject–predicate relations, relations between propositions, relational arguments in general, or even modal characteristics. Whether they are acceptable depends on how well they explain and clarify our spontaneous judgements about the arguments. They are not justified *a priori*, but by the same criteria we use for evaluating theories in the natural sciences, for example, explanatory power, simplicity and coherence with other beliefs. Logics also have predictive power, but they do not directly rest on observation since they are not first-order theories.

Peirce also holds that geometry and arithmetic are theories. They tell us what may be deduced from assumptions. In geometry, the assumptions are the axioms and the theorems the consequences. In arithmetic, they are rules of addition and subtraction, and how to form higher numbers from the digits 0 to 9. He also holds that numbers are properties of classes. (His example is that the number of New England states equals the number of sides of a cube, namely six, since the classes are similar in a certain respect.) Like Mill, Peirce rejects *a priori* justification. The difference is that Mill holds that the assumptions are inductive and not hypotheses, as Peirce does. The result is a theory of the deductive sciences that denies both that they are *a priori* and that they are inductive. We shall consider his argument against the *a priori* in the next section.

Quine's theory is an extension of Peirce's, although his philosophy of mathematics and theory of the relation of logic and arithmetic reflect more recent developments in logic and mathematics. He holds that sentences cannot be justified individually or even in theories, but that all of science must be evaluated as a unit. This doctrine is called *holism*. This calls for explanation.

Traditional empiricism holds that the theories of natural science and common sense move between two levels of unrevisable propositions. At the top are necessary truths, which are known *a priori*, and at the bottom observation or appearing statements. Necessary truths provide the framework for all science and are unchangeable and certain. They include propositions such as '5 + 2 = 7', 'The angles of Euclidean triangles equal 180 degrees' and 'Nothing can be *F* and not *F* at the same time'. At the bottom are propositions about how objects appear and reports of pains and sensations. These are contingent but can also be known with certainty because they are open to our direct inspection. Our access to truths at both levels is immediate and presuppositionless, that is, given in the sense discussed in Chapter 4. Common sense and science move between these levels, framing theories, making deductions by appeal to *a priori* truths and testing them by appeal to sensations.

Something like this theory is accepted by Descartes, Locke and Hume, as well as by the logical positivists of the twentieth century. In order for it to be consistent with empiricism, one has to hold that necessary truths have no basis in reality but are ideal, as Locke and Hume held. We have already discussed Sellars's argument that there is no empirical given, since all empirical beliefs rest on unconscious processes and presuppose other empirical beliefs. Mill held a similar theory on psychological grounds, while Peirce extended it by arguing that what seems to be direct acquaintance with sense data is actually abduction. For instance, when we perceive a robin, we appear to be directly apprehending an object in space, but are actually interpreting certain sensory cues on the basis of unconscious background beliefs about robins. The mode of inference is abduction and may be expressed as follows: if this is a robin, it will look a certain way; that looks this way, so that is a robin. The first premise is a background belief we may or may not be conscious of; the second is also usually unconscious (or immediate in Sellars's sense), but the conclusion is not.

Quine holds that the appearance of *a priori* insight at the top level is also illusory (again following Peirce, although on different grounds). First, he rejects necessary truths on the grounds that the claim that they are unchangeable and unrevisable cannot be clarified sufficiently to serve the purposes of a scientific philosophy. Secondly, he rejects the notion of analytic truth on the grounds that no plausible criterion can be given for when a sentence is true solely by virtue of its meaning. Theories are true by virtue of meaning and experience, but we cannot separate these components at the level of sentences. It is at this point that holism becomes a factor. Without an acceptable criterion of the analytic, synonymy or sameness of meaning, we must hold that our beliefs face experience as a *total theory*, any part of which may be accepted or rejected by making suitable changes elsewhere. Our total theory, he says, is "a man-made fabric which impinges on experience along the edges". When there is a conflict with experience, we have to reject some statements and limit the scope of others in order to incorporate the change because of the logical relations between the parts. Furthermore, the logical laws are themselves part of the theory and are also open to change, although they are closer to the heart of the theory and change more slowly. As a result, "it is misleading to speak of the empirical elements of an individual statement" and a mistake to look for a boundary between analytic and synthetic statements or those which hold no matter what and those based on experience. "Any statement can be held true come what may, if we make drastic enough adjustments elsewhere in the system" and "by the same token, no statement is immune from revision" (Quine 1961: §6).

If this is right, science and common sense do not operate between a fixed *a priori* realm and a realm of sense certainties. The difference between the three realms is a matter of degree with mathematics and logic at the heart and observation statements at the periphery. The only connection with nature is through observation and any statement is revisable in principle.

This raises issues that cannot be considered here. Quine's rejection of analyticity has implications for knowledge, since analytic truths have traditionally been the main examples of *a priori* justification. But analyticity is a semantic concept and his wholesale rejection of it is controversial (although no one has successfully answered his objections). Moreover, defenders of the *a priori* continue to accept the *a priori* and analyticity on the ground that both are indispensable, despite the problems. And his claims about holism and knowledge are mostly programmatic. These are important problems, but the issue here is the status of the *a priori* as a source of evidence.

The notion of the *a priori*

As we saw, *a priori* knowledge is presumably obtained solely by thinking. Furthermore, when we know something *a priori*, we know that it *must* be true. In thinking about the proposition '5 + 2 = 7', we have an insight that it is true and cannot be false. In simple cases, this insight is claimed to be self-evident where a proposition is self-evident if and only if it is perceived to be true as soon as we understand it. Reports of immediate experience are self-evident. When I see an apple, I know directly that something appears red to me, if I have the concept of red. And if I have the concept of green, I know that it does not appear green. Both propositions are self-evident, but they are not known solely by thinking; they depend on experience and so are empirical. When I consider the proposition '5 + 2 = 7', I know immediately that it is true, if I have the component concepts regardless of my experience at the moment. The awareness is analogous to my awareness of sensations, but is a perception of intellect, not the senses.

Two points should be noted about this account. First, it is not committed to holding that all *a priori* knowledge is immediate and self-evident. I may know that 12 × 6 = 72 immediately or I may have to work it out in my head: 6 times 2 is 12 and 6 times 10 is 60 and 60 plus 12 is 72. If I work it out, my knowledge of each step is immediate but my knowledge of the conclusion is not. (Recall Locke's discussion of demonstration in § "Knowledge and real existence", p. 21.) Yet the entire process is one of thinking and my knowledge is *a priori*, since none of the premises are empirical.

Secondly, the theory still allows experience to play a causal role. Experience is not required to justify a necessary truth, but it may still be needed to direct our attention to it. Russell says that all knowledge is caused by experience, but that some is *a priori* in that "the experience which makes us think of it does not suffice to prove it, but merely so directs our attention that we see its truth without requiring any proof from experience" (Russell 1959: 74). This is the sense in which *a priori* justification is independent of experience: the epistemic status of the proposition does not depend on experience, but is based on a positive insight independent of it. We *see* its truth, as Russell puts it, without requiring evidence from experience.

Objections to the *a priori*

Let us now consider some of the objections to the *a priori*. One is that appeals to the *a priori* are not certain. Geometers believed for two thousand years that parallel lines cannot meet no matter how far they are extended, but non-Euclidean geometries deny this without yielding contradictions, so claims that it was a necessary truth were mistaken. But this is not a serious objection. The question is whether there is a source of justification independent of experience. The fact that appeals to the *a priori* are fallible does not address this. We may have *a priori* knowledge even though every judgement is revisable, as Quine claims.

One problem in assessing this objection is that fallibility and necessity are often confused. If *a priori* claims are claims of necessity, there is a sense in which they cannot be mistaken, if they are true. Since a necessary truth cannot be denied without implying a contradiction, if we believe a necessary truth, our belief cannot be mistaken. This is true of simple necessities such as $2 + 1 = 3$ and complicated ones such as $126 \times 3 = 378$. They are equally necessary and cannot be false, even though few would claim to know with certainty that the second proposition is true. This is even clearer with higher mathematical truths such as $12,324 \div 12 = 1027$. This is also a necessary truth (I think) and cannot be false, but it does not follow that I know it to be true with certainty. This shows that there are two senses of infallibility. In one, a proposition cannot be mistaken if it is a necessary truth, no matter what our epistemic situation is with respect to it. This is the *modal sense* of 'cannot be mistaken'. The other sense is *epistemic*. A proposition cannot be mistaken in this sense, if I know with certainty that it is true. We can be mistaken about complicated necessary truths in this sense (such as $12,324 \div 12 = 1027$), since our evidence for them is not perfect; we may have made a mistake in calculating. We can even be mistaken about simple mathematical truths in this sense, since we cannot rule out the possibility that there is an evil demon tricking us. The same point holds on the traditional view of inferential *a priori* knowledge. We may be mistaken when we come to believe the conclusion of a proof by (presumably) intuiting the premises and each step in the deduction. We may mistake an error for an intuition at some point and be convinced that the conclusion necessarily follows when it does not.

Confusion of these senses has led philosophers down several false paths. Descartes holds that $7 + 5 = 12$ whether he is dreaming or not; hence the possibility that he is dreaming does not show that he does not know with certainty that it is true. But this assumes that $7 + 5 = 12$ is in fact necessary and is true whether he is dreaming or awake, that is, that he cannot be mistaken about it in the modal sense. But how does he know that it is? He may be dreaming at the moment he considers it. And since dreams cloud our judgement, it is possible that he is mistaken in the epistemic sense. In fact, once we make the distinction, it becomes plausible to argue that we may be mistaken in the epistemic sense about *any* proposition, since we cannot rule out the possibility of a demon deluding us. The point for the present discussion is that if such extreme fallibilism is at least discussable, we can hardly find fault with the claim that *a priori* judgements are not known with complete certainty.

The second objection is that mathematicians sometimes appeal to the *a priori* to support contradictory opinions and there seems to be no way to resolve the conflict. The usual reply to this is that if both sides pursue the issue in an unprejudiced manner, at least one will concede. As Ewing has put it:

> arguments may well be available which without strictly proving either side to be wrong put a disputant into a position in which he can see better for himself whether he is right or wrong or at least partially confirm or cast doubt on the truth of his view.
>
> (1962: 57)

This may well be the case, but it also may not be. The problem is that resolving disputes rests on the good will of the disputants and perhaps ultimately on whether a consensus forms on the question, but it is still the case, as Peirce pointed out, the *a priori* method does not have a reliable way of resolving disputes. But even if this is right, it does not follow that *a priori* insight is not a source of justification; it only follows that it is not a perfect guide to belief.

The third objection is that the main problem is the intelligibility of *a priori* insight. As we saw, apriorists hold that it is comparable to ordinary perception; it is "seeing" with the mind. Other terms also rely on perception: grasping, insight, apprehending. Even 'intuition' and 'self-evident' suggest analogies with sight. Brentano holds that we know that it is necessary that $3 = 2 + 1$ because we discover by reflection that it is *impossible* that three is not equal to two plus one, but he does not have a theory of how we know this except to say that it is an insight (Brentano

1969: 112). The usual reply to this is that, despite the unclarities, we cannot get along without the *a priori*. We shall examine this in the next section and concentrate here on the objections of Mill and Peirce.

They hold that apriorism confuses psychological and evidential factors, or, as it is often put, that it is guilty of *psychologism* (Peirce 1955: chs. 8, 20). 'Psychologism' is a label for two tendencies that logicians take to be errors about logic: (i) that logical principles are psychological laws or are based on psychology; and (ii) that the meanings of terms are ideas taken in the psychological sense as mental states. The first psychologizes logic and the second the theory of meaning. To this a third can be added: (iii) taking evidence and justification to rest on psychological states. Strains (i) and (ii) were dominant in the German logical tradition in the nineteenth century and were strongly opposed by Brentano, Husserl and Frege, while (iii) has been stressed by more naturalistic empiricists such as Mill and Peirce and implicitly by Quine. Brentano and Husserl, for instance, rejected conceptualism and the psychological view of logic, but continued to appeal to intuition. Frege resisted this early in his career, but eventually accepted intuition as well.

Let us look at this third version of psychologism. One form of it holds that inconceivability is a mark of logical impossibility and necessity (as Brentano held), that is, if we cannot conceive of a proposition being false, we know that it is necessary. Mill holds that whether we can conceive of something is a psychological fact about us and is not evidence of logical impossibility. For it to play an epistemic role, there must be independent evidence that it is a reliable indicator of impossibility and we can know this only on the basis of empirical evidence. The result is that our ability or inability to conceive of a proposition being true is no evidence of its truth value.

Peirce's objection is to intuition. He holds that appeals to consciousness are not evidential unless we can distinguish genuine intuitions from firm conviction. Without such a criterion, we have no reason to think the state is truth-conducive. When we assent to a proposition, we claim that it depicts a "real", that is, that its truth-value is independent of what anyone thinks about it. There are thus two aspects to belief: the subjective mental state of the believer and the intended object, which may or may not be part of the objective order of things. Like Mill, Peirce thinks that no matter how clear our "insight" is, it is not probative unless we have further evidence that it is truth-conducive. This evidence is either *a priori*, leading to similar questions at a higher level, or empirical, in which case the epistemic status of the belief rests on experience and is not *a priori* (see key point "Sellars on intellectual 'seeing'").

Peirce also has a second argument. Alleged intuitions are not presuppositionless, but are influenced by language learning and background beliefs even though we may not be able to detect their influence by introspection. Like those who accept the given in perception, the rationalist assumes that we have an intellectual faculty that does not presuppose structuring by experience. In a famous passage, Peirce says that the *a priori* method advises us to guide our beliefs by what is "agreeable to reason", but that this is itself subject to fashion and background influences, and so is not an independent source of evidence (Peirce 1955: 15–18).

Peirce's criticism may be put as follows. Defenders of the *a priori* hold that we can intuit certain propositions to be true independent of experience where intuition implies that the proposition is true and truth is independent of what anyone thinks about it. Intuition in this sense differs from belief, since believing does not imply truth, that is, '*S* intuits that *p*' implies *p*, but '*S* believes that *p*' does not. Peirce's objection is that there is no way to distinguish having a bona fide intuition from a mere belief. If asked why he thinks he intuits that $5 + 2 = 7$ rather than just believes it is true, the apriorist cannot argue that he sees that it is true. This begs the question, since the question is whether he sees its truth, that is, whether he intuits it. He also cannot answer that he intuits that he intuits it, since the same question arises about this meta-intuition. The result, Peirce argues, is that claims to have intuitions reduce to claims to have firm beliefs. The beliefs may be so strong that you cannot imagine that you are mistaken (in the epistemic sense), but from an epistemological point of view, this is just a firm conviction with no evidential value. Peirce's general conclusion is that all claims to know something by insight are abductive, that is, hypotheses, and have warrant only because they cohere with other propositions or result from reliable causal mechanisms. More may be said about this argument, but we shall have to leave the matter here.

Is the *a priori* indispensable?

Many philosophers argue that giving up the *a priori* comes at too high a price. They argue that it is needed: (i) to explain our knowledge of necessity; (ii) to answer skeptical objections to knowledge; and (iii) to do philosophy itself.

(i) As we saw, *a priori* insight differs from sensation in that it results in a judgement that something *must be* the case. It tells us that it is necessary and cannot be otherwise. In discussing this, we have to distinguish between knowing that *p* is true and knowing that *p* is necessarily true. We might come to know the truth of mathematical propositions by experience, but, according to the objection, this cannot give us knowledge that they are necessarily true. It seems clear that induction will not tell us this, but it does not follow that we could not have non-inductive theoretical reasons for thinking they are necessary. We might argue, for example, that mathematical and logical truths (e.g. 2 + 1 = 3 and the principle of the syllogism) are necessary because they remain true no matter what the content, even though our evidence for them is empirical, as Quine holds. To take an extreme example, a Platonist might argue that ethical truths are necessary because they assert relations between moral concepts that exist eternally, even though our only evidence for them is hypothetical and based on our pre-analytic moral beliefs. (The historical Socrates may have held such a view.) The result is that it is not clear that the *a priori* is needed to explain knowledge of necessity.

(ii) The claim that the *a priori* is needed to answer the skeptic rests on the argument that induction, sense perception and memory cannot be justified non-circularly on their own grounds. We cannot justify induction by generalizing from experience since all generalization presupposes it, and sense perception and memory cannot be justified without assuming their reliability elsewhere. We shall discuss these questions in Chapter 6, but even if they cannot be answered with appealing to the *a priori*, this is not likely to satisfy a competent skeptic. The *a priori* is subject to its own skeptical puzzles, which, it seems, can only be answered by holding that *a priori* insight is self-justifying, and this also begs the question.

(iii) Finally, what of the charge that philosophic argument would be impossible without the *a priori*? Aside from the air of desperation on which it trades, this presupposes a certain view of philosophy that empiricism without the *a priori* repudiates. If there is no *a priori*, philosophy's main task is not to certify our knowledge or some particular worldview, but to enlarge our understanding of it and our relations to it by framing hypotheses and supporting them by arguments from common sense and science. The objection presupposes that philosophy cannot be purely abductive, like the other sciences, but must be something more, and this is just what the rejection of the *a priori* commits us to. To the further objection that these arguments are themselves *a priori* and that denying the *a priori* is self-defeating, the answer is that they are not claimed to be *a priori* at all, but merely trace out the obscurities of *a priori* justification. If all interpretation, understanding and theory construction is hypothesis, philosophic analysis and criticism is itself hypothesis. This implies that philosophic conclusions cannot be certain and are revisable, but as we have seen, even defenders of the *a priori* have given up on this.

Summary

In this chapter, we have considered:

- the distinction between necessary and contingent propositions, and analytic and synthetic propositions;
- the problem mathematical propositions pose for empiricism and the responses of Locke, Mill, Peirce and Quine;
- the major objections to the *a priori*, especially by Mill and Peirce.

six

Empiricism and skepticism

Skepticism, fallibilism and empiricism

Critics often argue that empiricism cannot account for obvious cases of knowledge and so implies skepticism. In general, a skeptic about a certain domain of beliefs (e.g. the external world, induction, religious belief) denies that we have knowledge in that area. He need not deny that the propositions are true, but only that we cannot know that they are. He is also not committed to holding that we should not believe them. Skepticism is a purely epistemic judgement about the quality of our evidence. What might be called 'general skepticism' is the view that we have no knowledge at all, not even knowledge that we have none.

The question of skepticism obviously turns on the meaning of 'knowledge'. Traditionally, knowledge has been taken to imply that we cannot be mistaken in the sense that our evidence must be stronger than even the highest probability, so that 'probable knowledge' is contradictory. Since we no longer accept this, it is better to use 'absolute certainty' (or just 'certainty') for the traditional sense and take 'knowledge' to be the more inclusive term. To be certain that p is to be justified beyond all possible (i.e. imaginary) doubt, while to have knowledge is to be justified beyond reasonable doubt.

We can then distinguish four doctrines: *fallibilism* (the thesis that nothing is absolutely certain), *skepticism* (that nothing is known to be true), and their negations, *infallibilism* (something is certain) and what we might label *common-sensism* (something is known to be true). Since certainty implies knowledge even though the converse fails, these can

Skepticism:
Nothing is known

Infallibilism:
Something is certain

Fallibilism:
Nothing is certain

Common-sensism:
Something is known

- The opposite corners are contradictory: both cannot be true and both cannot be false.
- Skepticism implies fallibilism; infallibilism implies common-sensism.

be related on a square of opposition (see key point "A square of opposition"). The theses diagonally opposite each other are contradictories or negations and skepticism implies fallibilism, although the converse fails. Similarly, if we can show that something is certain, it follows that "common-sensism" is true and that skepticism is false. The important point here is that we cannot show that empiricism implies skepticism in a certain area because it implies that we are not certain about propositions in that area.

In this chapter we shall consider three skeptical problems that face empiricism: the problem of the external world, the problem of justifying basic sources of empirical knowledge on empiricist principles and the more general problem of showing that our categories correspond to reality.

Locke and the veil of perception

The problem of the external world may be put in terms of the following argument:

(1) All knowledge of physical objects rests on experience.
(2) Experience does not provide knowledge of physical objects.

Thus (3) We have no knowledge of physical objects.

The first premise follows from empiricism. The second is based on three interconnected arguments.

- First, when we perceive the world, we are aware only of various contents of experiences such as shapes, colours, sounds and tactual impressions, and there is good reason to believe that these are not identical with the surfaces of physical objects. Hence we cannot know directly that a present experience is a perception of a real object and not a figment of the imagination.
- Secondly, we cannot deduce the object from sensations, since it is possible to have similar experiences when no objects are present, for example, in dreams and hallucinations.
- Thirdly, we cannot know by induction that an experience is caused by an actual object, since induction is restricted to what we can experience and we are only aware of our ideas or sensations.

If we are to avoid the skeptic's conclusion, we must reject one of the premises. We must reject (1) and give up empiricism or reject (2) and find a way within experience to show how we can have knowledge of external objects.

The problem is this. If we start from the assumption that the mind directly perceives ideas or sense data caused by physical objects, how can we get beyond them to knowledge of external things? This can be illustrated as follows:

$$\text{Mind} \xrightarrow{\text{directly perceives}} \underset{\text{sense datum}}{\text{Idea}} \xleftarrow{\text{causes}} \text{Physical object}$$

The mind directly perceives ideas, which are caused by physical objects, but we cannot deduce the objects from them. We also cannot infer them by induction, since we are only aware of the datum side of the relation and never of the object side. The result is that the physical world is unknowable on empiricist principles. This is often put by saying that ideas, that is, sensations and their contents, form a veil of perception between us and the world, which leaves the world a mystery, if indeed there is one.

This is usually thought to be fatal to Locke's empiricism. He held that ideas represent real physical objects, but, according to the standard interpretation, also took ideas to be entities standing between us and them; hence the problem of the veil. While Locke clearly held that we directly perceive ideas that represent real external objects (a view we may call *representative realism*), it is not clear that he accepted this theory of ideas. For there to be a veil of perception (or an iron curtain, to use another image), ideas must be existences, something like pictures behind which objects lurk, and it is not clear that Locke holds this. He thinks that ideas are perceptions when taken as existences, but fictions when taken as representations of physical objects. Perceptions are acts of mind with certain contents, but the contents are not separate existences. Only the perceptions are real entities. When we see an apple, we perceive a round reddish shape, but Locke thinks it is a mistake to reify this shape. 'Red' and 'round' describe the kind of perception we have; they do not describe an object with independent existence between us and the apple. Locke's ontology recognizes only particulars (whether minds or material objects) and modifications of them. A perception is a modification of the perceiver's mind and has its own peculiar character that we can think of without thinking of the mental state; this is the idea taken as a content or thought-object. If the apple exists, the perception is not an illusion and its object is a real particular in addition to being an object of thought, but if it does not, there is only the perception; there is no idea that exists distinct from the perception. We talk of ideas (as modifications of perceptions) as if they were real entities, but, according to Locke, this is only a manner of speaking.

This may be explained with an analogy. A player gets a home run in baseball when he hits safely and touches all four bases without the help of an error. When he does this three times in a game, we say that he had three home runs, but home runs are not things like the ball and the bat. Talk about home runs is a short way of describing certain kinds of turns at bat. They do not exist separately from the batter hitting the ball and running the bases safely. Similarly talk about ideas as thought-objects is just a convenient way of talking about kinds of perceivings that animals undergo and does not commit us to holding that they are existences that shield us from physical objects.

This view of ideas was common in the seventeenth century and dates back to the Middle Ages. The scholastics held that we can consider a perception ('intention' in Latin) in two ways: "subjectively" as a mode of thought or modification of the perceiver, or "objectively" by concentrating on what it is about, that is, its object. But there is only one entity, the perception itself, considered in different ways. This derives from a grammatical ambiguity of the genitive in Latin and English. The phrase 'picture of the king' may refer to a picture the king owns or what it is about. In the first sense, the genitive is subjective and in the second objective. Similarly, 'Book of Ruth' refers to the biblical book *about* Ruth, while 'Book of Matthew' refers to the book *by* Matthew. Background knowledge makes these phrases clear, but sometimes this is not possible (as in 'the Word of God'). Perceptions taken as mental states are states of perceivers and are subjective, but are objective when taken as what they are about, namely, objects common to many perceivers. (This is the origin of the modern distinction between 'subjective' and 'objective', according to which the first refers to the private state and the second to the public object it represents.)

Ideas taken in this way differ from sense data. As we saw, Russell holds that sense data are objects of acts of acquaintance *and* exist independently of them. As a result, if representative realism is correct and sense data are not identical with physical objects, there is a barrier between us and the world.

Whether Locke accepts this conception of ideas may be debated, but it is clearly an option for the empiricist. He can hold that when we have an external perception, we have a sensation that has an *intentional object* that may or may not be real. If the perception is veridical, the object is real and if it is illusory (such as a dream or hallucination), it is a fiction immanent to the perception. The doctrine of representative perception may then be reinterpreted as holding that when a perceiver has a sensation of O, he cannot determine from the sensation alone whether O is real or only a figment. At best, the proposition that O exists (e.g. that there is an apple) is a hypothesis that is justified because it coheres with other beliefs (or if we accept reliabilism, because it results from a reliable perceptual mechanism).

Some metaphysical alternatives

Let us leave Locke's theory aside and take *representative realism* to be the doctrine that we directly perceive sense data, which we take to represent real physical objects. In this sense, the doctrine posits a "twofold existence" in ordinary perception (as Berkeley described it) and so is more clearly subject to the veil-of-perception objection. Hence if we are empiricists, we must reject the second premise of the skeptic's argument and make physical objects accessible to empirical evidence. One way empiricists have done this has been to offer metaphysical alternatives to representative realism, which reduce physical objects to sense data, which are clearly within our experience. Another strategy has been to reject sense data altogether and hold that we directly perceive substantial physical objects. Let us consider these in turn.

Phenomenalism, idealism and direct realism

The metaphysical theories empiricists have offered to solve the problem are phenomenalism and idealism. *Phenomenalism* holds that physical objects are not material substances, but bundles of sense data. Since sense data are directly perceived, it follows that they are within the orbit of experience. Instead of holding that physical things cause sense data, phenomenalism holds that they are reducible to sense data so there is no veil between them and us. There are not three realms of entities – minds, phenomena (i.e. sense data) and physical objects – just minds and phenomena. This transforms the problem from avoiding skepticism to explaining appearance and reality within the realm of sense data. The strategy is that if we cannot have direct contact with the world, reduce the world to what we do have direct contact with or, as the leprechaun in *Finian's Rainbow* sings, "When I'm not near the girl I love, I love the girl I'm near".

Berkeley's *idealism* can be considered a version of phenomenalism. The essential feature of phenomenalist theories is the reductionist thesis, but a further question is the ontological status of the phenomena themselves. Berkeley holds that they are ideas and hence that physical objects are systems of thought-objects that have no existence independent of minds. A phenomenalist need not go this far. He might accept the reductionist thesis without committing himself on whether sense data are ideal or real, and consider this to be a separate issue. The result is an empiricist alternative to skepticism that remains agnostic on the question of idealism. Or the phenomenalist might reject idealism and take sense data to be real entities, that is, entities that are independent of what is thought about them. The result would be a phenomenalist realism. Using the terminology of sense data, we can distinguish two theses:

(i) Physical objects can be reduced to sense data (the *reductionist thesis*).

(ii) Sense data are dependent on the thought of some mind (i.e. they are Berkeleyan ideas).

The idealist accepts both (i) and (ii), the phenomenalist realist accepts (i) and denies (ii), the phenomenalist simplicitur accepts (i) and makes no commitment on the truth of (ii). Berkeley held (i) and (ii), John Stuart Mill held (i) and rejected (ii), while others (perhaps A. J. Ayer in the twentieth century) accepted (i) and hedged on (ii).

What these theories have in common is *the thesis of direct perception*. They hold that we directly apprehend physical objects in ordinary perceptual experiences, and so know directly when they exist where direct apprehension is a form of acquaintance, that is, when S directly apprehends an object, S directly knows that it exists. The result is that direct perception yields non-inferential knowledge that physical objects exist.

We may put the phenomenalist response to the veil problem as the following argument.

(1) Physical objects are reducible to sense data.
(2) Sense data are directly perceived
Thus (3) Physical objects are directly perceived.

Premise (1) is the reductivist thesis and (3) the thesis of direct perception, while (2) is taken to be an obvious thesis accepted by all parties, including skeptics. But, as one would expect in philosophy, what one party takes to be obvious, another considers hopelessly mistaken. This leads us to the third empiricist alternative to the veil of perception: *direct realism* or what its defenders like to call *common-sense realism* (and its critics *naive realism*). This holds that (3) is true (we directly perceive external objects), but both premises are false, since there are no sense data. Whereas phenomenalism solves the problem by collapsing the data–object dualism to sense data, direct realism collapses it by claiming that there are no sense data. Thomas Reid, a younger contemporary of Hume, and his followers argue in this way, holding that the direct perception of physical objects is a basic principle of common sense. Ideas and sense data are fictions created by philosophers and, according to them, the skeptical problem does not arise from physical objects being inaccessible, but from philosophers mistakenly positing intervening entities between us and them. The ordinary person (they claim) holds that physical things are substantial material objects and finds it ridiculous that they are systems of sense data or are screened from us by intervening entities.

The problem with direct perception

What are we to make of these theories? Since our focus is on epistemological questions, we can avoid the metaphysical problems that arise over reductionism and idealism. But all the theories face problems over direct perception. The ordinary person may think he is directly aware of physical objects, but this does not answer the skeptic so easily.

The problem is that a single experience does not show that a physical object exists. Most interesting external objects have what Hume called "continued existence." They do not exist just when we perceive them, but exist at least for a short time before and after. A single experience, however, only establishes that the object exists at that moment. Whether it existed a moment ago rests on memory of a past perception or, when we look away then look back, on hypothesizing its existence in the interval. And whether it will exist a moment later can only be known when the moment arrives, or inferred from a past perception. Direct perception at best shows that they exist in the present and not that they exist before or after. When I directly perceive O at t_1, I know that it exists at t_1, but this does not show that it existed at t_0 or will exist at t_2, since O's existing at t_1 does not entail that it exists at another time.

It might be objected that a single experience does justify us in thinking the object is real. As J. L. Austin remarked (1962: 48–9), we can all tell the difference between actually being introduced to the pope and dreaming that we are. The perception has a clarity and vivacity that surpasses a dream, and this difference is immediately present to us. But this does not show that the belief in continued existence is non-inferential. We interpret the experience as a non-dream because of its clarity and this interpretation is a hypothesis, not something we directly know to be true. The judgement must be a hypothesis since a single experience does not *guarantee* that the object persists no matter how vivid and clear it is.

This is confirmed by what common sense holds about physical objects. It holds that they have four characteristics: (i) they are *individuals* with determinate properties (a specific mass, shape and colour); (ii) they have sides, a back and a bottom, and so are *spatially complete*; (iii) they have *causal properties* that allow them to interact with other objects and cause us to perceive them; and (iv) they *endure* for some length of time. Clearly we cannot immediately know that an object in front of us has all these qualities from a single glance. The most we can know is how it looks at that moment from that perspective. That it is substantial, has a back, causal properties and endures are hypothesized. The clarity of the experience at best shows that this hypothesis is justified and not a wild guess.

If this is right, the problem is not that there is a veil of perception, but that physical objects transcend what we can know at any given moment from perception. The skeptical problem persists whether we take the object to be "behind" our sense data or move them up to be directly present to the mind, either as systems of data or as substantial physical things. Whichever view we accept, all we can know in a single perception is there is an entity at that moment; the rest is inference. The problem also exists if we interpret Locke's theory of ideas as suggested in the previous section. According to this, a sensation has an intentional object that may be ideal or real, and we cannot tell which solely by examining it. Since real physical objects have continued existence, the belief that the object is real is at best a conjecture. This is what Locke had in mind when he argued that sensitive knowledge is a non-demonstrative inference from our intuition of how the object appears to its reality. It is always possible for the premise to be true and the conclusion false.

The problem of transcendence is a plague on all houses and not just an objection to representative realism. Nor is it empiricism's problem alone. It infects rationalism as well. We shall consider whether the problem shows that we have no knowledge of external objects after we have examined the other arguments skeptics have offered to empiricism.

The general problem of the external world

We have been concentrating on knowledge of specific physical objects, given that we only directly perceive sense data. But there is also a more general problem of the external world, namely, how we can know that there is an external world at all. There are thus two questions:

- How can I know that my present experience is of a real physical object?
- How can I know that there are any physical objects at all?

The first asks how we can know whether a given experience is veridical or illusory. The second asks how we know whether *any* experiences are veridical: is our experience as a whole a dream or not? These are separate questions. We may be able to answer the second without being able to answer the first, that is, know that there are external objects without knowing that we are now perceiving one. On the other hand, if we could answer the first, we would also have an answer to the second. We have been dealing with the skeptic's claim that we cannot answer the first. Let us briefly consider the second.

Most empiricists have admitted that we cannot be *certain* that there is an external world and have taken it to be a hypothesis, but there is still a range of opinion on the issue. At one extreme, some have held that it is an article of faith that cannot be justified without begging the question. A more moderate view is that it is a reasonable hypothesis, or, as it is sometimes put, the best explanation of our experience. At the other extreme is the view of idealists and direct realists such as Berkeley and Reid that it is not a hypothesis at all, but something we can be certain is true because we directly perceive it.

Hume's view is typical of the first view. He holds that "men are carried, by a natural instinct or prepossession, to repose faith in the senses" and that without any reasoning suppose that there is an external universe that would go on existing "though we and every sensible creature were absent or annihilated". He thinks all animals are "governed by a like opinion" (*EHU*: XII i 151). George Santayana's term for this was "animal faith" (1955: ch. XI). We do not know it by argument, but believe and act on it by instinct. Santayana and presumably Hume agree that we cannot refute a determined skeptic since we cannot prove conclusively that there is an external world. The result is that it is a blind article of faith that has no intellectual authority, but one that we cannot avoid.

Russell's view in 1912 was less extreme. He agrees that belief in an external world is instinctive, but thinks it is a simpler explanation of our experience than other theories (e.g. phenomenalism, idealism and the mystical belief that the whole of life is a dream). By positing substantial entities, realism provides a locus and cause of our appearances: they are different views of a single system of things in a common space. Phenomenalist theories take physical objects to be systems of sense data with "a hole in the center" whereas realist theories posit an unperceived core that causes the data. We do not have detailed concepts of the nature of this core. We can only know it by description as "the cause of our data". He does not explicitly say so, but this suggests that he considers realism more rational than other theories (Russell 1959: ch. 2).

The more extreme theories of Berkeley and Reid that the external world is not conjectural may be more plausible initially, but, as we have seen, direct perception does not live up to the claims made for it. This is especially damaging, since they base the rationality of the belief in an external world on it. Berkeley goes so far as to claim that direct perception provides an absolutely certain guarantee of common sense against the skeptic. Let us look at his account more closely.

He says that the representationalist is forced to the conclusion that "we cannot attain to any self-evident or demonstrative knowledge of the existence of sensible things", but this doubt vanishes once we take them to be directly present to the mind. "I can as well doubt my own being, as of the being of those things which I actually perceive", since it is contradictory that the objects of direct perception can be independent of thought (*PHK*: §88). This claims that we know with certainty that physical things exist. But the argument for this is not clear. He might mean that he knows it with the same self-evident certainty he has about his own existence because he can intuit when he is being presented with a real thing, but this is clearly mistaken. As we saw, the most he can claim is that the present object *appears* to be a real thing rather than a phantom.

On the other hand, he might be basing his certainty on his general idealist argument that unconceived physical objects are impossible, but this also fails. The most this shows is that realism is false, that is, that there are no unperceived objects. It does not show that the perceived objects that remain are real in his sense, namely, forced on him by a superior power. All he knows from the present experience is that some ideas cannot be willed away. As Hume later pointed out, our perceptions may be self-caused by an inner power, caused by a superior mind or caused by non-mental physical objects, and we cannot know which is the case from the fact that they are not within our control. Other defenders of direct perception have made similar claims to know with certainty that there is an external world (e.g. Reid), but they seem to have confused (absolute) certainty with intense conviction and need not be considered here.

Rationalists in general have found this a scandal and have sought refuge in the *a priori*. Kant argued that we can infer from the very fact that we are aware of appearances that there must be a world of things in themselves, since 'appearance' implies something of which it is an appearance. But this is not convincing. The argument turns on describing the intentional objects of our experience as appearances and we have no ground for using such loaded terminology. If we use a neutral term such as 'sense data', we cannot make any inference to external objects, since being a sense datum does not imply that there is anything of which it is a datum.

A more famous (and interesting) argument is Descartes's. Appealing to *a priori* principles and his idea of God, he argues that our natural inclination to believe in an external world cannot be mistaken, since God's perfection is inconsistent with deception. Unfortunately, this argument is unsound even if we accept Descartes's rationalist theory of knowledge. He takes it to be self-evident that a perfect being would not deceive him about external reality. But perhaps God has a sense of humour and thinks that tricking him would teach him humility. It would surely make a fine practical joke if only God and Descartes existed. One might also ask how God could not have a sense of humour, given that he is perfect and made us in his image. We might even argue on Cartesian principles that our having a sense of humour *shows* that the creator must have one as well, since a sour-puss could only create sour-pusses. Once again Descartes makes an assumption and confuses it with an *a priori* principle.

There is also something humorous about the argument. As Hume noted, to appeal to God's veracity to prove the veracity of our senses is "surely making a very unexpected circuit", for once we call the world in question, we are "at a loss to find arguments" to prove God's existence at all (*EHU*: XII i 153). Starting from empiricist (and common-sense) assumptions, Hume finds it incredible that anyone would think that God's existence is more certain than the existence of an external world, for example, that it is more doubtful that there is mutton on the table than that God exists.

The result seems to be that we cannot "satisfy our reason" that belief in an external world is true, as Hume put it. It is an ineluctable assumption for which no good argument can be given and the best we can hope for is that it is not a grand illusion. We shall have more to say about this later.

Induction, perception and memory

Another problem facing empiricism is the validation of the basic sources of evidence. If asked how you know something, you might reply that your doctor told you, that you learned it in school, that you read it in the newspaper, or that your psychic told you. These are specific sources that you take to confer credibility on your belief. You might also answer the question more generally by saying that you know it by experience (or reason). One of the tasks of epistemology is to evaluate such sources. A preliminary list of the sources that provide informative general rules might be:

- external perception
- introspection (Locke's "inner sense")
- testimony
- memory
- induction, deduction, abduction
- reason (the source of *a priori* knowledge).

The first three can be taken to make up experience, but testimony seems to be derivative. You must be able to hear or read what the witness or expert tells you, and, it would seem, in addition have evidence that he is reliable. Memory is also not an original source. If you remember something, you either remember seeing it or have learned it from some other source. Memory preserves beliefs from the past and enlarges what we know personally, but does not provide basic evidence. Induction, deduction and hypothesis move us from one set of beliefs to another and are inferential sources. Reason may be taken to include deduction and *a priori* intuition of basic premises. The basic sources of empirical evidence, then, would seem to be perception, memory and induction. Perception provides the basic premises, memory preserves them and induction is the method of generalization.

Calling these sources of evidence or knowledge suggests that they are causes of knowledge. This is true, but they also provide us with basic epistemic principles, the application of which enhances the evidential status of beliefs. We may say, for instance, that seeming to remember a proposition increases its warrant under certain conditions. Similar principles can be constructed for the other sources. The result is two sets of problems for the epistemologist:

- What are the grounds for thinking that these principles are true?
- What are the exact conditions under which seeming to remember, perceiving or introspecting, or inferring it from another proposition enhances a proposition's status?

We have already discussed the *a priori* and will discuss testimony for miracles in Chapter 7, but otherwise a detailed discussion of the second question is beyond our scope here. The first question, however, is pertinent to the issue of skepticism and its relation to empiricism.

The central problem is circularity. To justify a source, we must appeal to another source that we assume, justify it by yet another source or proceed in a circle. To take a simple case, if asked how you know that you are awake, you might pinch yourself or ask your neighbour whether you are awake, but these beg the question. You might dream that you are pinching yourself or talking to someone. The problem is more complicated when you try to justify an epistemic principle rather than a specific belief, but is the same in principle. To justify perception, the most promising line would be to show that your spontaneous perceptual beliefs result from a reliable perceptual mechanism, but this can be shown only by further appeals to perception, which is circular. The argument also appeals to induction and memory and this raises further questions. One is the problem of justifying induction. But induction also assumes data to start from and this, it seems, must come from perception. Furthermore, to have sufficient data, we need memory, which can only be shown to be truth-conducive by further appeals to perception, induction and remembered data. The best we can do, it seems, is to assume the reliability of perception, memory and induction, and hope for the best.

Rationalists often argue that the *a priori* can accomplish the job along the lines suggested by Descartes's perfect-God argument, but, as we saw, this is a failure. We might try other *a priori* strategies, but the concept of the *a priori* is too obscure to satisfy even the most modest skeptic. Without a theory of how conceptual insight differs from firm belief or a vague feeling of obviousness, the rationalist is left with promissory notes, but no solution.

Kant offered a more modest solution along rationalist lines. Instead of arguing directly that perception, memory and induction (and other sources) are reliable, he argues that their reliability is a necessary pre-condition of knowledge. By this he means that, unless they are justified, we have no knowledge of external facts at all. The problem is that this turns on an ambiguity about justification. Showing that a method is required for knowledge does not show that it is reliable, but justifies it only in the weaker sense that we have no other option but to accept it. The skeptic might agree to this and still reasonably doubt that it produces knowledge. At best, Kant shows that we are not to be blamed for accepting these sources. The epistemologist wants to learn whether they are truth-conducive and will lead to true beliefs in the long run. Kant's argument does not address this question.

In fact, Kant's solution is not very different from Hume's. Hume holds that all three sources are based on custom and habit, and that we have a natural instinct to follow them. They are presuppositions of knowledge, like our belief in an external reality. He thinks skeptical arguments have only a momentary effect on us and do not make us tranquil, as the ancient skeptics held, but agitated and depressed, but this soon passes, especially if we engage in other, less intellectual activities. We shall look at Hume's view more closely below in § "Empiricism and common sense" (p. 133).

Further problems: the new riddle

A third skeptical problem for empiricism is Nelson Goodman's "new riddle" of induction (Goodman 1955: 74ff.). We believe that emeralds are green because all the emeralds we have examined have been, but

Goodman notes that we can also invent artificial predicates that are equally well confirmed by this evidence. Suppose we define 'grue' so that x is grue if and only if x is green up until a certain date, say, 1 January 2050, and blue thereafter. All the emeralds we have examined until now are both green *and* grue, and induction will not eliminate the grue hypothesis until we get to mid-century, but we can always invent other grue-like predicates by choosing different times. We can also concoct an infinite range of bleen predicates (bleen: blue before tomorrow and green thereafter). Goodman's claim is that there is an infinite number of these "funny" predicates consistent with our empirical evidence no matter how large it grows and we cannot determine whether emeralds and other things we think are green are not actually grue or have some similar predicate. Goodman calls predicates that can be projected across *all* times *projectible* predicates. His question is how we can determine whether our predicates are projectible or not.

Goodman calls this a "new riddle" of induction because it introduces a new set of possibilities that cannot be eliminated by inductive procedures. In what sense is it new? From the beginning there have been two problems of induction. One is Hume's problem of justifying some inductive rule. The second is the problem of applying the rule. The principle of induction states that unexamined instances will resemble examined ones, but this is clearly not a universal truth. At best *some* unexamined cases resemble examined ones. The second problem is the problem of providing criteria for when we can extrapolate from observed cases. The new riddle is an instance of this second problem. If we had criteria for when a predicate is projectible, we could tell when generalizing from data is sound and when it is not.

When we look at it in this way, Goodman's problem has been a problem for empiricism from the start. As we saw in Chapter 1, Locke distinguishes between the concepts we use in investigating the world (the "nominal" essences) and the natural kinds in the world (the "real" essences). His question is how we can determine which invented essences (the nominal ones) correspond to the real ones. He thinks this question is unanswerable and doubts that we shall ever discover the real essences of things. Whether this and Goodman's problems are problems of induction, they are clearly problems for empiricist theories, which hold that all knowledge of reality rests on experience and induction.

The problem can be put in the following way. When we investigate nature, we always begin with a background theory about the predicates that can be combined to form laws as well as principles about the relations between the predicates and their relevance to one another. Colour, for instance, is not thought to be as relevant to a creature's genetic heritage as its shape or size. The role of induction is to discover which of these predicates are connected in lawlike ways. If this is right, induction starts from a general assumption about the possible structure of the world and refines it through experience. But, as Locke held and the new riddle shows, it cannot justify this general theory. The best it can do is to eliminate hypotheses about the correlations between the predicates.

What are we to make of this problem? One proposed solution is Descartes's theory of innate ideas. He thinks we have innate ideas that represent the general structure of the world (including its geometry) and that God's veracity guarantees their correspondence. Some remarks by Hume suggest that he might hold a similar theory. He says that there is "a kind of pre-established harmony between the course of nature and the succession of our ideas". Although "the powers and forces" of nature are unknown to us, "yet our thoughts and conceptions have still, we find, gone on in the same train with the other works of nature" (*EHU*: VI ii 54–5). He is talking about his problem of induction, but his remarks can be extended to the new riddle and Locke's problem. But he does not think this harmony, if there is one, is a direct result of God's action; it has a natural explanation and is not a direct gift of God.

Some have thought that evolution can solve the problem. The harmony Hume speaks of can be explained because it has survival value. Creatures without innate propensities to think in harmony with nature would not have survived. This may be the correct explanation, but it does not answer the skeptic who wants a justification for thinking our basic concepts are adequate. First, evolutionary theory is itself an empirical theory based on induction and other empirical theories, so that appealing to it is circular. Secondly, even if we could get around this, natural selection still does not show that our conceptual scheme corresponds to the ultimate structure of reality. It might justify the concepts we use at the practical level (avoiding dangerous animals, not eating certain plants and finding mates), but there is no reason to think it prepares us for dealing with ultimate questions such as the origin of the universe or the constitution of the smallest particles. The result is that our belief that our concepts are adequate in a way that Goodman's "funny" predicates are not is another supposition of knowledge we cannot justify. We may have natural propensities to believe in an external world, follow induction and trust perception and memory, and also to frame adequate concepts for thinking about basic questions, as Hume argues, but we cannot validate them without begging the question or making assumptions elsewhere.

Empiricism and common sense

The conclusion we seem to be driven to is that empirical knowledge (and perhaps all knowledge) rests on assumptions we cannot justify without circularity. Some have taken this to show that the skeptic is right after all, since his main claim is that we cannot give a fully rational account of knowledge. But this is not skepticism in the sense we have been taking it. We have to distinguish between skepticism as the denial of knowledge (our sense) and as the denial of knowledge that we have knowledge. The latter is clearly a stronger thesis. We might have knowledge even though we cannot show that we do. Hume, for instance, holds in the *Enquiry* that we have knowledge, even though he denies that we can prove that we do. In the passage in which he claims that there is a harmony between our beliefs and reality, he says that unless there is such a harmony, "our knowledge" would be "limited to the narrow sphere of our memory and senses" (*ibid.*). He obviously denies that we have to show that we have knowledge in order to have it.

The issue between these two senses of skepticism is the problem of *externalism* and *internalism*. As we saw, externalism holds that we can have knowledge provided our basic assumptions are true even if we cannot justify them non-circularly, or, to put it another way, knowledge can rest on assumptions we cannot discharge. An internalist theory denies this and holds that knowledge must be fully validated and cannot rest on any assumptions. The stronger conception of skepticism is internalist and rejects Hume's theory (in the *Enquiry*) without argument. (It should be noted that Hume was more sympathetic to the stronger conception in the *Treatise*.)

The internalist argues as follows:

(1) If our beliefs cannot be fully justified, we do not have knowledge.
(2) Our beliefs cannot be fully justified.
Thus (3) We do not have knowledge.

where to *fully justify* a belief or theory is to justify it without arguing in a circle or appealing to undischarged assumptions. Premise (1) is the thesis of internalism. Hume and his internalist critic might agree that (2) is true, but Hume rejects (1). He thinks we can have knowledge even though it rests on undischargeable assumptions.

It is often argued that (1) is the traditional notion of knowledge, but this is inconclusive, since the externalist's position is that the traditional notion needs replacing. It also cannot be defended by counter-examples, since it can be argued that they are effective only in so far as they reflect the traditional account of knowledge.

A stronger argument is that externalism opens the door to superstition, since it allows us to adjust our assumptions to justify whatever we wish to believe. Although it is not usually recognized, Hume has a reply to this. He holds that rationality in "common life" is defined by what we can defend by appeal to the three basic sources; we assume these are reliable and require that all other beliefs and sources of empirical evidence (testimony and authority) be justified in terms of them; and superstition cannot meet this test. He does not think this conception of rationality is *a priori*, but that it is implicit in our ordinary interaction and social life, that is, in "common life". The internalist holds that *all* beliefs must be justifiable without appeal to assumptions (although he is not usually also worried about circularity, unless he is a skeptic) and that nothing should be accepted on faith unguided by reason and evidence. Hume is sympathetic with this, but exempts induction, perception and memory (and our belief in external reality) on the grounds that our acceptance of them is instinctual. He thinks we should restrict our basic assumptions as much as possible.

Hume calls his view *mitigated skepticism*. Its major claim is that we have a natural propensity to rely on induction, memory and perception. The skeptic's strongest arguments are the veil problem (which Hume clearly recognized), the problem of induction and the impossibility of validating perception by experience. We cannot answer these by appealing to other evidence, since induction and perception are the source of *all* evidence from experience and we have no independent evidence of external objects. The result is that we cannot make any headway against the skeptic on these issues. But Hume thinks this cannot affect our practice, since our belief in these basic principles cannot be swayed by argument. "Nature is always too strong for principle." Even the skeptic cannot be convinced by his own arguments; "the first and most trivial event in life will put to flight all his doubts and scruples" and he will continue to make inferences even though he cannot satisfy himself about "the foundation of these operations" or answer the objections to them (*EHU*: XII ii 160). Excessive skepticism of this kind cannot have any effect on us.

But he thinks there is a weaker form of skepticism that is instructive and useful to society. It makes two recommendations. First, we should not be too "affirmative and dogmatical" in our opinions, but hold them with "a small tincture of Pyrrhonism" and realize that there are always "counterpoising" arguments. Secondly, we should limit our enquires to subjects within our cognitive capacities and avoid questions that are beyond us (*EHU*: XII iii 161–2). To this may be added a third: all beliefs about matters of fact should be based on experience so far as possible. These admonitions are not moral rules, but characteristics of "just reasoning" that distinguish the wise from the vulgar.

Hume calls this a version of skepticism, even though he assumes in the *Enquiry* that we have knowledge and holds that we cannot fully justify its basic principles. How do these claims go together? His view is that the failure to give a full justification does not imply that we do not have knowledge. We might agree with him on the other aspects of mitigated skepticism, but it is not clear that it is intellectually respectable to claim knowledge without a fully satisfying justification.

One attempt to answer this question was made by G. E. Moore. He holds that arguments to show that we have knowledge "must be of the nature of a *petitio principii*". Anyone who tries to show that he knows some external facts must appeal to "some instance of an external fact which he does know", and this begs the question (Moore 1959: 159–60). This can be generalized. We cannot disprove the skeptic's claim that there is no knowledge by argument, since he will not accept our premises unless they are known and this is the point at issue. Furthermore, if we claim that we know intuitively that we have knowledge, the skeptic will demand a reason for believing that this is a genuine intuition and not just a firm conviction, and this calls for a criterion for making the distinction, a criterion that must be justified in turn. The result is that we cannot refute skepticism by proving that we have knowledge.

But this does not mean that we have to agree with him. For any argument the skeptic gives, Moore says: "It would always be at least as easy to deny the argument as to deny that we do know external facts" (*ibid.*). Moore's point is that when confronted with an argument for a conclusion we reject, we can reject the validity of the argument or one of its premises rather than accept the conclusion. In the case of the standard skeptical arguments, Moore thinks it is more reasonable to reject the argument than to deny knowledge. Even if we cannot show that our common-sense assumptions are true, we can still rationally reject the skeptic's arguments against them. It might be argued that the skeptic's arguments rest on obvious premises, but this is not an argument the skeptic can give. If he did, he would be committed to having knowledge and so contradict himself. In fact, the skeptic cannot give any arguments at all. The most he can do is to show that the non-skeptic accepts certain claims that are not consistent with his claim to have knowledge (on the basis of his own rules of consistency). And this leaves it open to the "dogmatist" to adjust his assumptions to meet the objection just as Moore suggests.

To see how Moore's strategy works, consider the argument that there is no knowledge since knowledge implies absolute certainty and nothing is known with certainty. This can be schematized as follows:

(1) Knowing that p implies absolute certainty that p.
(2) Nothing is known with absolute certainty (the thesis of *fallibilism*).
Thus (3) There is no knowledge (i.e. *skepticism*).

Fallibilists accept (2), but this does not commit them to (3), since they can always reject (1), as Moore suggests. In fact, this seems to be what happened historically. The ancient skeptics argued that the claims of the Stoics and Platonists (the "dogmatists", as the skeptics called them) that knowledge implies certainty commit them to the impossible task of showing that our beliefs are infallible. When the debate was renewed in the modern period, the non-skeptics weakened the requirement and accepted the possibility of fallible or probable knowledge rather than give up the claim that we have knowledge. Since it is a common-sense belief that we have knowledge, they preferred to weaken the conception of knowledge than contradict common opinion.

We can also apply Moore's strategy to the internalist argument that knowledge cannot rest on undischarged assumptions. We can reject the requirement that basic sources must be fully justified, that is, justified non-assumptively and non-circularly, as Hume does in the *Enquiry*. He adopts an externalist position and holds that knowledge rests on ineluctable suppositions. Although the point is controversial, this seems to be the most plausible way for empiricism to defend itself from skeptical arguments we considered earlier. When faced with an argument that his doctrine implies skepticism, the empiricist should look for some flaw in the reasoning or for a premise (or background assumption) that can be rejected rather than accept the conclusion. If he can do this, he can avoid skepticism without giving up his empiricism. But we must be careful not to overstate the implications of this. Without direct arguments that we have knowledge, our belief that we do is based on assumptions and so is an article of faith. Moore's strategy is a delaying tactic; it allows us to defend common sense from its critics, but our acceptance of it is still assumptive.

Despite his caution in other respects, Moore seems to overstate his case on this point. After admitting that he cannot disprove the skeptic's conclusion, he says: "The only proof that we do know external facts lies in the simple fact that we do know them" (Moore 1959: 160). If externalism is right, we do know them *if* our assumed sources are reliable, but it is misleading to say that it is a *simple fact* that we know external facts. We believe we know them, but Hume would undoubtedly caution against being overly affirmative about this; we may not know it at all, since our belief rests on an assumption.

Moore's strategy also throws light on the problem posed by Goodman's new riddle (and Locke's doctrine of nominal essences). In addition to assuming that there is an external world and that induction, perception and memory are reliable, we assume that the outlines of our theory of the world are true, even though we can imagine alternatives to it and admit that significant modifications might be necessary in the future. Goodman is clearly right that we cannot justify our basic concepts by induction. Our classificatory system is a background theory we bring to specific experiences and is based on abduction rather than induction. It is also less central than our belief in an external world or trust in the basic sources. The history of science (and common sense) shows that our concepts change in significant ways, so that it would not be rational to take our present scheme as fixed.

The reason is that the background theory has significantly more content than the belief that there is an external world. The claim that there is an external world asserts only that our ideas are caused by non-mental things. It does not give us a detailed picture of them or the laws that govern them. All we have of it is a relative idea with minimal content. The theory of how it is structured is given by our conceptual scheme, which operates as the most general theory of its outlines, and we know that this is subject to adjustments. It is here, I think, that Hume's advice that we should proceed "with a tincture of Pyrrhonism" (*EHU*: XII iii 161) is pertinent. Whereas our beliefs in an external world and the reliability of the basic sources are fixed points of common sense, our confidence in our categories should be more tentative.

Summary

This chapter has dealt with:

- the problem of justifying claims about physical objects and the existence of an external world in general on empiricist principles;

- the responses to the problem offered by representative realism, phenomenalism (in both its realist and idealist versions) and direct realism;
- Goodman's "new riddle" of induction and its relation to Locke's doctrine of nominal and real essences;
- the externalist implications of Hume's claim that knowledge rests on assumptions we cannot justify non-circularly and Moore's method of dealing with the problem.

seven

Empiricism and religious belief

We have been examining some of the problems faced by empiricism: the nature of experience, the *a priori* and skepticism. In this chapter, we shall turn to the application of empiricism to religious belief. As we have seen, all of the empiricists reject *a priori* arguments for the existence of God, such as Descartes's argument that he must exist because he is infinitely perfect and existence is a perfection. Hume's response to this is typical of empiricists. He says that "there is an evident absurdity in pretending to demonstrate a matter of fact, or to prove it by any arguments *a priori*", since "Whatever we conceive as existent, we can also conceive as non-existent" (*DNR*: IX, 189). But this is not the most interesting application of empiricism to the question. The main epistemic question is whether there are empirical grounds for beliefs about God's intentions. We shall consider three arguments: (i) the argument from design, which claims to prove that the universe was created by an intelligence; (ii) the argument that we can know his intentions from religious books such as the Bible or Koran because they report miracles that can be supported by empirical evidence; and (iii) arguments from religious experience and mystical states. The first three sections will deal with design, Hume's criticisms and the effect of Darwin's theory of natural selection on the question. The following two discuss revelation and Hume's criticism of the rationality of miracles, and the next deals with religious experience.

The argument from design

The argument from design may be summarized as follows:

(1) The universe and its parts exhibit design and order, for example, the planets, the eye, animal reproduction.

(2) Order results from either chance or a designer.

(3) It does not result from chance.

Thus (4) It results from a designer.

(5) Design implies an intelligence with goals and plans about means.

Thus (6) There is an intelligence who designed the world, that is, God.

The first premise is known by experience. Premises (3) and (5) are also empirical: we know from experience that parts do not arrange themselves into complex objects by chance but require an intelligence to organize them.

The most prominent exponent of this argument is William Paley (1743–1805) (Paley 1963: chs 1–3). He thinks it has three advantages over other arguments. First, the evidence for (1) is empirical and cumulative. As we learn more about nature we will discover more instances of design, strengthening the evidence for (1). He thinks the complexity of the eye or ear proves the conclusion by itself, but that multiplying instances makes it even more convincing (*ibid.*: 33). Secondly, if this is right, scientific progress will strengthen the argument, and there will be no conflict between science and religion. Finally, it does not just prove that there is a cause of nature, but that he is an intelligent being with goals. Other empirical arguments (such as Aquinas's) claim to show that there is a first efficient cause or an unmoved mover, which we call God, but leave a gap between what they prove and the characteristics we normally associate with God. This argument closes the gap.

Paley illustrates the argument by comparing the universe to a watch (*ibid.*: chs 1–2). He says that if you found a stone while crossing the heath, you could easily conclude that it had lain there forever. But it would not be reasonable to think this if you came across a watch. A watch's parts are put together to produce motion, which is "so regulated as to point out the hour of the day". Each part has to work in harmony to produce the result: the box containing the spring, which transmits the motion to the fusee, then to the balance and the pointer with an intricate system of small wheels. If any of these were in a different place, it would not serve its purpose. Paley holds that nature is full of similar instances of design that together point to a creator of great power and wisdom.

Paley adds several remarks by way of clarification. First, we would think the watch was designed even if we had never seen one before and had no knowledge of how it works. We know that it is a designed artefact because of its complexity, not because of our knowledge of watches. Furthermore, we would come to this conclusion even if we discovered that it generated itself. In fact, this would make the conclusion even stronger since a watch that generates itself would have to be considerably more complex than an ordinary one.

Secondly, we cannot avoid inferring a designer by positing an infinite chain of causes. If the watch was self-generating, we might hold that the one on the heath is simply the result of other watch "parents" whose lineage goes back to eternity. But this does not explain the central fact, namely, that the watch's parts are arranged for a purpose. We want to know what caused the contrivance itself and positing an infinite chain of causes does not explain this. It is not the existence of this watch that needs to be explained, but how such complicated machinery can produce such a useful effect, and this requires a designer outside the series of causes. "A chain composed of an infinite number of links can no more support itself than a chain composed of a finite number of links" (*ibid.*: 9).

Thirdly, we might hold that there is no skill in designing the watch; the parts just happened to fall into place by chance just as three rocks in a brook or the parts of the stone happen to be arranged as they are. Paley says this is what the atheist holds about nature, but he thinks it is an unreasonable position. Chance might explain why the watch is face down in the dirt, but it cannot explain how the parts came together in just this way in order to give the time. Further, the atheist's claim that all the parts of nature (from the movement of the planets to animal organs) result from chance strikes sane people as incredible, especially when we take into account the inner mechanisms on which the outward properties depend.

Taken together, Paley thinks this shows that there must be a first cause and that the universe could not come about by chance. It must have been designed and created by an intelligence.

In the next two sections, we shall consider Hume's criticisms of the argument on logical grounds, and the challenge posed by Darwin's theory of natural selection in the nineteenth century, which threatened to reintroduce the conflict between science and religion by explaining the main instances of design on naturalistic grounds by chance.

Hume's criticisms

Hume criticizes the argument on three grounds: (i) despite what its proponents claim, there is still a gap between what the argument shows and the conclusion about God; (ii) if the universe requires a cause, we might also ask for a cause of God; and (iii) despite appearances, the argument does not tell us anything about God's intentions towards us. The first reintroduces the gap problem and the second the infinite regress, while the third threatens to undermine the religious significance of the argument.

(i) The gap between the argument and its conclusion

Hume claims that the argument is too quick in concluding that the organizing agency responsible for nature is God. When we infer hidden causes from observed effects, we must "proportion the power of the cause to the effect" and be careful not to attribute more to the cause than we find in the effect. For example, if we are shown a scale with a known weight on the raised pan while the other tray is concealed from view, the most we can reasonably infer is that the hidden weight is just enough heavier than the observed one to raise it. It may be a great deal heavier, but we cannot tell this by observation. If the known weight is x, the most we can infer is that the other weight is x plus whatever is needed to tip the scale. We also cannot tell whether the hidden tray has one weight on it or several, or what their specific weights are (*EHU*: XI, 136).

Hume argues that this shows that the argument goes beyond the evidence in concluding that the cause of order is a God similar to that of the great religions. First, we cannot infer that the designer is infinite in power or intelligence, but only that it has enough power capacity to create this finite world. The argument also does not show that there is only one designer and builder. For all we know, there may be a god who planned the universe and another one who constructed it, so it does not support monotheism over polytheism. Philo, the skeptic in Hume's *Dialogues Concerning Natural Religion* (*DNR*: V), considers some of these possibilities.

- We know that ships and buildings are built by many men working together, so it would be reasonable to think that many gods worked on the universe. We also do not know that this is the only world he created. "Many worlds might have been botched and bungled, through an eternity, ere this system was struck out:

Much labor lost: Many fruitless trials made: And a slow but continued improvement carried on during infinite ages in the art of world-making" (*DNR*: V, 167).

- We might admit that "the universe sometime arose from something like design", but we cannot "ascertain one single circumstance" beyond this on which to base a theology. We tend to think the universe is perfect, but, for all we know, it may be "very faulty and imperfect, compared to a superior standard". It may have been "the first rude essay of some infant Deity, who afterwards abandoned it", or of an inferior god who is "the object of derision to his superiors", or perhaps the work of "old age and dotage in some superannuated Deity" who has since died leaving it to continue on from the impulse he gave it (*ibid.*: V, 169).

We can multiply these possibilities. The universe might have been created by a committee of gods of varying ability, similar to a government committee, in which the geology god (the one controlling earthquakes) was less competent than the anatomy god in charge of body parts such as eyes and reproduction. Another possibility is that a family created the world and the imperfections were the handiwork of the children. As Hume says, these possibilities cause "signs of horror" in the faithful (*DNR*: V, 169). The point is that the argument hastens to a conclusion that supports our usual religious beliefs, but falls short on close examination. The result is that there is a gap between what it proves and the God of the Abrahamic religions.

(ii) If the universe requires a cause, we might also ask for a cause of God

There is also a problem about the infinite regress. Philo, Hume's spokesman, argues in *Dialogues Concerning Natural Religion* (part IV) that the skeptic can as reasonably ask what caused God as the theist can ask what caused the order of nature. (God is as much in need of an explanation as the order of nature.) Cleanthes (who defends the argument) replies, "I have found a Deity; and here I stop my enquiry. Let those go farther, who are wiser and more enterprising." Philo's response is that naturalists hold that this "ideal system", that is, God's plan, is "not a whit more explicable than a material one", that is, God and God's plan are no more or less self-explanatory than nature itself (*DNR*: IV, 164–5).

Although the issue is complicated, there is something to Cleanthes' view. He wants to explain the order of nature; to ask for an explanation of God raises a further question he is not required to answer. But there is still a problem. Cleanthes thinks the world needs an explanation, but God does not, while most atheists hold that the world does not need an explanation. Both sides agree that explanation cannot go on indefinitely; they differ on where we should stop in providing one – and it is difficult to see how this question can be decided. John Hick says that the theist claims that the world needs an explanation to be rendered rational, but this assumes that it requires a rational explanation and the non-theist denies just this (Hick 1983: 23).

(iii) The argument tells us nothing about God's intentions towards us

Hume also has a third objection. In the *Enquiry Concerning Human Understanding*, he discusses the argument in an imaginary dialogue with a friend who is trying to defend philosophy from critics who claim it has harmful effects. Theism argues that design not only proves the existence of an intelligent creator, but that he created it with our happiness in mind; and that he will redress the injustices in the world by rewarding the good and punishing the wicked in an afterlife. Hume's "friend" argues that this illicitly infers an effect from a feature of the cause that is not supported by evidence. The design argument infers a cause from an effect, then moves from the cause to explain a new effect, but this is reasonable only if we know enough about the cause to infer this. To explain an effect from an unfounded feature of the cause "must of necessity be a gross sophism" (*EHU*: XI, 141). This is a variant of the principle behind the scale example: we cannot infer further detail in the cause than we can observe in the effect.

Hume's point (put in the mouth of his "friend") is that it is illegitimate for the theist to infer details about God's plan (such as how he will deal with the injustices of this life) from the order of the universe, since nothing we can observe in this life shows this. The theist imagines himself in God's place, then reasons that God would act as he would. But there is no evidence for this. If we have no evidence about his intentions about the matter, we cannot say how he would act.

The principle behind the objection is that if A is postulated as a cause on the basis of observed characteristics X and Y, we are entitled to infer that A has the power to bring about X and Y, but we cannot reasonably infer that he also has the power to bring about an unobserved effect Z. The evidence may show that the creator is a designer and builder, but it does not show that he also has a more elaborate plan that includes an afterlife.

Hume raises a possible reply to this in the dialogue with his "friend". If we see a half-finished building with mortar, stones and tools nearby, we can reasonably infer that the builder has further plans for it and will return to finish it. Similarly, when we perceive one footprint, we can reasonably infer that a two-legged man was walking on the beach and that the water washed away the other prints. The theist can argue that the universe is like a half-finished building and the designer has "a more finished scheme or plan" in mind that he will finish at a later time (*EHU*: XI, 143).

Hume offers two replies to this, one given by his friend and one by Hume himself. First, it is reasonable to make the inferences in the case of the footprint and the building because we have evidence for causal laws relating them and their causes, but we have no evidence for how a deity would act in the case of the universe. We know that footprints are made by human beings with two legs, so we know that there must have been others that have vanished. But if we did not have any background beliefs of this sort, but only saw this single footprint, we could not reasonably tell how it got there. For all we know, it might have been made by a one-legged bird or by a long-legged animal taking a single step from one rock formation to another. Hume says (through his "friend") that the theist's argument is more like this case. "The Deity is known to us only by his productions, and is a single being in the universe, not comprehended under any species or genus, from whose experienced attributes or qualities, we can, by analogy, infer any attribute or quality in him" (*EHU*: XI, 144). We can infer wisdom and goodness in him just so far as the universe shows it. But we are not authorized to infer "farther degrees" of these attributes "by any rules of just reasoning".

The second response is this (given by Hume himself): the only way we can make just inferences from single events is to consider them under "known species" that we know by experience are conjoined with other events. But God and the creation of the universe are both unique and cannot be related to other beings and events by causal laws. Although he leaves the reader to draw his own conclusion from this, the result would seem to be that any talk about God's creation must be completely speculative.

This last point is often taken as evidence that Hume thinks that all talk of God is meaningless since he is unobservable. This is how the logical positivists and defenders of "the Old Hume" interpret him, but we have to be cautious here. If '*p* is meaningless' is taken to mean that *p* is neither true nor false, this is not Hume's view. He holds that 'God exists' and 'God created the universe' have a truth-value, but that we cannot know what it is. He is skeptical about claims about God in the sense discussed in Chapter 6: the propositions may be true, but we can never know "by just reasoning" whether they are or not. Hume sometimes suggests the stronger view. He says, for instance, that the concept of God is unintelligible, but he does not mean by this that it is completely devoid of content. For a concept to be intelligible in his sense, we must be able to defend attributions of it from objections, that is, it must be clear and precise enough for us to be able to tell when it correctly applies. This is the sense in which the claim that causation is necessary connection is unintelligible, according to one interpretation of Hume's account of causation. The concept is not devoid of content, but is too unclear to be useful in philosophic discussion.

Chance and design

The most serious challenge to the argument is not philosophic (and logical) but scientific. Paley's conviction that science would strengthen the argument proved to be mistaken. In 1859, Darwin's theory of natural selection explained the biological instances on the basis of chance without positing a designer. Roughly, Darwin held that species change over time, but remain mostly the same, that is, offspring resemble their parents but not completely. These variations occur by chance; and those that give the creature an advantage in adapting to the environment have a better chance of being passed on to the next generation and spreading throughout the species. Furthermore, geology and archaeology tell us that there has been life on earth for several billions of years so that chance has had an enormous time in which to operate. If this is right, we can explain complex and highly adaptive organs such as the eye and the ear on the basis of chance and natural processes. The theist's claim that only a designing intelligence can explain the biological instances of design is false.

This is often taken to support atheism, but this is a mistake. Natural selection shows that design is not the only explanation of the complexity of species. This undermines the argument from design, but it does not show that there is no intelligent creator. The point can be explained in Thomistic terms. Aquinas held that God is the *first cause*, and that natural agents and processes are *second causes*. Darwin's theory explains species and their characteristics on the basis of second causes and chance, but it does not show that there is no first cause. The argument from design accepts development within species, but not across species, while Darwin's theory explains how new species can develop positing only chance and second causes. It moves divine agency further into the background, but does not deny it.

I will not discuss the scientific merits of Darwin's theory here, but will focus on the objection that it is not a reasonable alternative to intelligent design, since chance still cannot explain life as we know it. Theists argue that an organ such as the eye could have come about by evolution only if a great number of chance variations occurred at just the right time and in the right order; and the odds against this are incredibly high, so high that the result could occur only if an intelligent agent were guiding it.

Hume was aware of this objection and, since he was writing a century before Darwin (and the new geology), accepted it. In fact, his statement of the objection is a classic. He puts it in the mouth of Philo, the skeptic in the *Dialogues Concerning Natural Religion* and presumably his spokesman (*DNR*: XII, 215). Philo says the ancient physician, Galen, says that there are 600 different muscles in the human body each of which must be adjusted in one of 10 different positions to perform its function. The result is that in the muscles alone more than 6,000 "views and intentions must have been formed and executed" to get them to work together. In addition, Galen says that there are 284 bones with 40 different functions. Philo exclaims:

> What a prodigious display of artifice, even in these simple and homogeneous parts? But if we consider the skin, ligaments,

> vessels, glandules, humours, the several limbs and members
> of the body; how must our astonishment rise upon us, in pro-
> portion to the number and intricacy of the parts so artificially
> adjusted?   (*Ibid.*)

If we magnify these chance occurrences as we must if Darwin is right, the coincidence of them all occurring in the proper temporal order is astonishing.

This has an initial plausibility, but it rests on a fallacy. It calculates the probability of events after they have happened, while probability can only be applied before events happen. If you are dealt thirteen spades at bridge, you might marvel at the improbability of it and think some god of cards was looking out for you, but this is a mistake. Any particular hand of thirteen cards is equally unique (since there is only one card of each value and suit in a fifty-two-card pack), so that if a perfect spade hand is cause to marvel, any hand you get should be equally marvellous. If you predicted that you would get thirteen spades (or any other specific hand) and turned out to be right, the event would then be marvellous. The odds against you are so great that the other players would prob-ably accuse you of cheating. But once you got the hand without having made the prediction, you cannot wonder at the improbability of it. The chance of getting just that hand after the fact is 1, not some enormously small fraction of 1.

Another example is this. There are roughly three billion US one-dollar bills in circulation, each with a unique serial number. If I find one in my wallet and claim that a wondrous marvel has occurred, I would be considered mad. The odds against my predicting that I would get just this bill are 3 billion to 1 and, if I did it fairly, it would indeed be a wonder. But if I do not predict the serial number, the probability that I got this bill with this number is 1; since I have it, it is not just highly probable (in the mathematical sense) that I got it, but certain. The same is true of the second dollar bill I find. Even though the odds of my correctly predicting that I would pull out just these two bills are $1/3,000,000,000^2$, an astounding improbability, the probability after the event is 1.

The theist's (and Philo's) objection commits just this mistake. When we figure the probability of human beings and other animals being as they are now, the probability is 1. If we assume that our present state was intended in the beginning, then the fact that we are here now cannot be explained without an intelligent designer, but this begs the question. If chance alone was operating, we are the result and it is just superstition and vanity to think that some being wanted us to come about. This is why people who get perfect hands in bridge think they have been favoured by the gods: they think that their success at cards (and in life) is important in the scheme of things, but there is no reason to think that it was not just luck. Similarly, our existence now is just good luck (or bad luck, depending on how you view it), if Darwin's theory is right.

There is also a second point to be made about the objection. At any stage in evolution, the probability of some new development is based on the options available *given that level of complexity*. The probability that the creature is at just that stage at that time is 1. In calculating the probability of predicting the next stage, it is an error to include probabilities we would have calculated at earlier times to get to this stage. We do not consider *all* the probabilities from the beginning of time. That would be like considering the probability that you have just this coin out of the millions in circulation when you calculate the probability of getting heads in flipping it now. The probability that you will get heads with the coin is 0.5, since the probability that you have this coin rather than some other is 1 and 1×0.5 is 0.5. Philo and critics of natural selection commit this error when they bunch together all the probabilities at each stage and multiply them to show how absurd the theory is. If e has occurred, its probability is 1 and if the probability of the next event occurring (before it has occurred) is p, the probability of both events occurring is $1 \times p$ or just p. (The point can be illustrated by an old joke. A woman carries a bomb on a plane. When asked why, she says, "I was worried about terrorists and what are the chances of there being two bombs on a plane?")

The objection also begs the question by assuming that the present state of the universe was intended. If the hypothesis of chance is correct, it was not the result of anyone's intention, but just happened. We intelligent beings are here to discuss the question, but it could also have happened that there was no universe at all or that the dominant creatures were dinosaurs. At the first moment, all of these were equally incredible and perhaps even equiprobable. It is because we are here thinking about it and have such a high regard for ourselves that we think we must have been the intended outcome of the process. But if the chance theory is right, this is just vanity. Poets sometimes extol the beauty of human beings, the symmetry of their bodies and faces, with matching arms, breasts and legs, and one nose and mouth with balanced eyes and ears; but this is not because we match some ideal form. If we had noses on our left hip and eyes on our wrists, we would be equally astonished at how marvellous it is that we were made in just this aesthetically pleasing way rather than as deformed beasts with eyes, noses and mouths as we have them now.

Faith, reason and miracles

The classic account of faith and reason is by Thomas Aquinas (1999: pt. I). He holds that reason includes what we can discover by our natural abilities, while faith is above reason in this sense. Reason can discover that God exists, is eternal, good, omnipotent and all-knowing, and that he has a plan for the world and us. But it cannot establish the specific truths of Christianity, such as the Trinity (that God is three beings in one: the father, son and holy spirit) and that Jesus came down to earth to relieve us of original sin. These can only be known because God revealed them to us through the Bible.

A similar view is defended by Locke, but with some significant differences. He agrees that faith is above reason, but disagrees about which is dominant. Aquinas holds that we should always follow faith when faith and reason conflict. Locke argues that we can believe something on faith when it is incompatible with *probable* belief, but not when it is incompatible with *demonstrative* reason. That is, a doctrine is not a proper candidate for faith if reason can show with certainty that it is false. As a result, when faith and reason tell different stories, Aquinas believes that we should follow faith, whereas Locke holds that we should follow faith only when the evidence for the belief is probable. His argument for this is that if God revealed a tenet that contradicted demonstrative reason, he would be undermining the most useful gift he has given us.

Locke also puts greater emphasis on determining when faith is genuine. The central problem of faith is determining when a doctrine is an actual revelation from God and when it is what Aquinas calls a "foolish fable". Aquinas holds that miracles are the criterion. Christians have true faith, while Islam is just a fable. His argument is that the survival of Christianity against overwhelming odds is a miracle, while Islam survived because Mohammed promised his followers many wives in paradise. Locke agrees that miracles are the criterion, but offers a detailed theory of how "reason guides faith" and seems to make faith a compartment of reason.

Locke distinguishes between faith and what he calls "enthusiasm". Faith is belief *above reason, but guided by it*, while enthusiasm is belief *above reason and not guided by it*. The enthusiast's beliefs may be true, but they are irrational, since he has no evidence that God revealed them.

As Locke says, the enthusiast's beliefs are not based on reason and evidence but arise from "the conceits of a warmed or over-weening brain"; he is convinced that he is right because God revealed it, but has no evidence to show this. Locke seems to be motivated by the fear that enthusiasm (irrational faith) will lead to intolerance and have detrimental effects on society (*Essay*: IV xix 7).

The following argument shows how revelation can indirectly support an article of faith:

> Whatever God reveals is true.
> God reveals that *p*.
> Thus   *p* is true.

We may grant the major premise on the ground that God does not lie. The problem arises with the second. How are we to know what he has revealed? The traditional way is to appeal to religious writings, which we can show derive from God because of the miracles they describe. One of Locke's examples is:

> (A) The angels rebelled against God.

Since this is not contradictory, it is consistent with demonstrative reason and so is a candidate for revelation. We also cannot support it directly by probable evidence since we have no witnesses or physical traces of the rebellion. But we can indirectly base it on reason by the following argument:

> (1) Whatever God reveals is true.
> (2) History shows that the biblical miracles occurred.
> Thus (3) The Bible is God's revelation.   (From (2))
> (4) The Bible reports that (*A*) is true.
> Thus (5) (*A*) is true.   (From (1), (3) and (4))

Locke thinks (1) is true *a priori*. He also thinks we have good empirical evidence for (2) and (4), that we can infer (3) from (2), and that (1), (3) and (4) imply (5). It is thus rational to believe on faith that the angels rebelled. If we cannot give this or a similar argument based solely on reason, but believe that the angels rebelled anyway, we are enthusiasts and our belief is irrational.

Locke justifies his position by appeal to the Bible itself. He says that God proved that the Ten Commandments were from him by talking to Moses through a burning bush, that is, by producing a miracle. And when Moses still had doubts (he did not believe just any burning bush), he turned Moses' staff into a serpent. Hence Locke argues that his account of faith is condoned by the Bible itself. He does not think the story proves his theory, since it would be circular to appeal to the Bible in order to show its reliability. His aim seems rather to be that he cannot be reasonably accused of heresy or atheism if he is only following Moses' example and basing faith on miracles.

Several points should be noted about Locke's (and Aquinas's) theories. First, they assume that God's existence can be proved by reason independent of faith. Without such a proof on natural grounds, all faith would reduce to enthusiasm or foolish fables, since miracles presuppose that God exists. Religion may tell a consistent story, but there would be no way to get beyond its claims to show that the story has a foundation in fact.

Secondly, the evidence for miracles must also be based on reason. Otherwise, they cannot be used to distinguish between genuine and bogus faith. We also cannot just appeal to the Bible as evidence for them and so as evidence that it is God's revelation. That would be like believing a salesman when he assures you he is honest. (Groucho Marx once said that if someone tells you he is not a crook, you know you have one on your hands.) There must be independent grounds to show that the Bible is the true word of God in contrast to other counterfeit religious works.

Thirdly, Locke's approach seems to destroy the distinction between faith and reason by insisting that religious belief be reasonable. In order to accept something on testimony, even the testimony of God, we have to have evidence (i) that the witness is reliable and (ii) that the witness said what is claimed. In the case of God, there is no question of his reliability, but there is a question whether the Bible is his testimony. If we believe without evidence that it is, we believe what might be a foolish fable. It is not a question of trusting God, but of knowing which of the competing claims to be the testimony of God is from him. This is presumably why Moses asked for confirmation: the burning bush might have been the devil attempting to lead him astray.

A final point: why was Locke so quick to accept God's word as true? We have no guarantee that what he tells us is true, since we have no way of knowing his intentions. For all we know, deceiving us might enable him to carry out his overall plans more perfectly. Perhaps Locke's reason for accepting (1) was that, no matter what we say about this issue, determining what he has revealed is still a central problem.

Hume and miracles

If Locke is right, the question of the true faith turns on human testimony and miracles. The most famous discussion of this is Hume's essay on miracles in the *Enquiry*. He holds that a miracle is a violation of a law of nature, which we can know was caused directly by supernatural intervention because laws cannot be altered by human beings. A human being can make a burning bush appear to talk by clever stage magic, but only God or an agent of God could make it talk. As Aquinas said, a miracle is an event that occurs "out of the order of nature", by which he meant that it cannot result from second causes or nature, but must come directly from the first cause. Hume states his position as follows: When presented with a miracle:

> I weigh the one miracle against the other; and according to the superiority, which I discover, I pronounce my decision, and always reject the greater miracle. If the falsehood of his testimony would be more miraculous, than the event which he relates; then, and not till then, can he pretend to command my belief or opinion.   (*EHU*: X i 116)

Hume's position is that it is always more reasonable to reject testimony to a miracle than to believe that a law of nature has been violated; thus, it is never reasonable to accept a miracle. There are two interpretations of this. The standard one is that he believes that, when we balance the evidence for the law holding against the evidence for the witness's reliability, the law always wins, so the rational conclusion should always be that no miracle occurred. A second interpretation is that Hume holds that we know as a general rule that testimony to miracles is defective and hence do not have to weigh the evidence for and against it in each case. We may call the first the *balancing interpretation* and the second the *rule interpretation*.

According to the balancing interpretation, Hume's point is that we should reject the "more miraculous" alternative where this is taken to mean the one for which we have less evidence. His claim is that, when we do this, it is always more reasonable to think the law was not violated and reject the testimony. The rule interpretation holds that his argument is that the more miraculous alternative is always that the law has failed, since it is a law of nature and there is no law that witnesses always report the truth. Thus, when we consider the failure of the law against the failure of the testimony, it is more reasonable to think the testimony has failed, since the law always wins in a contest between a law and a non-law.

This issue cannot be considered in detail here. Aside from textual evidence, one argument in favour of the rule interpretation is that it gives a more sympathetic reading of Hume. There are clear counter-examples to the balancing argument that do not apply if he is defending a general rule. Hence, in the spirit of the general topic, we should accept the more charitable interpretation.

One such counter-example is this. Suppose the odds of winning the lottery are 20 million to 1. If the newspaper says that your friend has won, you would believe it even though the chances against him winning are considerably greater than the chances that the paper made a mistake in reporting the winner. In this case, it is more reasonable to accept the *less* likely alternative and Hume's general principle that we should always reject the less likely one as false. But this is not a counter-example on the rule interpretation, since your friend winning a lottery is not a miracle. To use Hume's terminology, it is a marvellous event but not a miraculous one. A marvel is an unusual event or one we would not expect, but it does not violate any laws. Believing your friend won is not believing that a miracle occurred and Hume's principle that we should always accept the least miraculous event does not apply.

One might wonder why the rule interpretation undermines the reasonableness of miracles. Two factors are relevant. First, Hume argues that the criteria for good testimony rest on generalizations that fall short of being laws. We know that nervous or uncorroborated witnesses are less reliable than confident ones who are supported by other evidence. We also distrust witnesses who tell exactly the same story or have an interest in the outcome. But there are no laws that state the conditions under which they are not mistaken. As Hume notes when considering why miracles never happen in our own time: "it is nothing strange, I hope, that men should lie in all ages" (*EHU*: X ii 120). All sorts of misrepresentation are possible: witnesses may misperceive, misremember or be deceived by a clever illusionist posing as a holy man, or they may be lying. This is true even in the case of saints. Although we can be assured that they would not lie for their own benefit, they might well do it for our benefit. (Indeed this might be expected of saints.) The result is that the falsity of testimony is never a miracle, and it is always possible in any given case that the testimony is in error.

Secondly, it is a mistake to think that believers in a miracle are balancing the testimony against the law. Since they are claiming a miracle, they are committed to holding that the event violates a genuine law, and we can explain its occurrence only by supernatural intervention. If they were balancing the testimony against the law and opting for the testimony, they would be rejecting the law and so not claiming that a miracle occurred. Their view is that the law of nature continues to hold when the event occurs, but that God suspended it in order for the event to occur. They do not claim that the alleged miracle refutes the law, since this would imply that there is no law and no miracle. It is at this point that Hume's argument applies. His general rule is that there is always a reasonable doubt about the testimony, but none about the law being genuine. Thus it is always more reasonable to believe that the testimony is in error and that no miracle occurred.

Hume claims that this is a rule we follow in our daily affairs. Suppose a witness at a trial testifies that he saw a bird fly into the room, turn into the defendant, kill the victim, then turn back into a bird and fly out the window. No one would believe him, no matter how sane and credible his testimony has been in the past. It is only in religious contexts that we lower our standards in order to accept miracle stories supporting our own beliefs. In non-religious contexts and when the stories support religions we reject, we follow Hume's rule. In rejecting the reasonableness of miracle stories, Hume is in effect advising his countrymen to apply the same standards on Sunday that they employ doing business with each other the rest of the week.

It is important to note that Hume does not hold that miracles are logically impossible. The proposition 'Miracles exist' is not contradictory and so is a matter of fact. But it also cannot be known to be true, since, according to his empiricism, matters of fact can only be known on the basis of empirical evidence and the argument we have just been considering shows that it is never rational to believe a miracle. A second point is that Hume's argument is not *a priori* but empirical. It rests on the fact that there is no law governing the reliability of testimony. If there were such a law and we could certify witnesses who report a miracle as reliable under it, we would have an actual case in which we would have to weigh one miracle against another, since we would have to pit two violations of laws against each other. But that is not the case in our world.

A criticism often made against Hume is that we usually have no good explanation of how the testimony went astray. The best we can do is conjecture what went wrong and this is not enough. Paley says that if ten impeccable witnesses told the same story of a miracle without consulting each other and even after they had been tortured, we could not explain their testimony and how it failed to be true. Yet Hume holds that we should reject it and deny that the miracle occurred. But this is not a sound objection. Their testimony does not show that the event occurred, but only that they *believe* it did. But more importantly, having a reasonable doubt does not commit you to explaining the fact some other way. It only justifies you in not accepting the explanation given. A jury can have a reasonable doubt about a defendant's guilt without having any idea who did the crime. Hume does not need a specific and plausible explanation of how the testimony came about in order to reject it as unreasonable. As he once wrote: "Does a man of sense run after every silly tale of witches or hobgoblins or fairies, and canvass particularly the evidence? I never knew any one, that examined and deliberated about nonsense who did not believe it before the end of his enquiries" (quoted in *DNR*: 49 n.2). This is not dogmatism, but common sense, Hume would argue.

The argument from religious experience

Many people claim to know God by direct experience. They feel his presence, he advises them; or he appears to them in a more spectacular manner, such as a blinding light, as he reportedly did to Paul on the road to Damascus. Such experiences are religious experiences, that is, *experiences in which one senses the presence of a superior spiritual being.* They (i) have a *noetic quality* so the subject comes to believe that the being is present, but (ii) are not necessarily veridical, that is, the belief they generate might be mistaken. They are also said to be ineffable, especially when they are so momentous as to be life-changing. But this is not essential since it is usually possible to describe them by analogies and metaphors.

Locke has a famous discussion of them. He calls them *original revelations*, since they are directly from God, whereas revelation through a third party, for example, a prophet (such as Moses), a book (such as the Bible) or a religious tradition, is *traditional revelation*. Locke makes two points about original revelation. First, it is not self-authenticating. The subjects claim to have a "clear light" and "an awakened sense", but they cannot determine whether the cause is God, Satan or "a warmed and over-weening brain". Until they can, the belief may be mistaken "however it be called light and seeing". "I must see that it is God that reveals this to me, or else I see nothing." The strength of their conviction is "no evidence at all of their own rectitude" (*Essay*: IV xix 10–11). Secondly, to answer this question, the subject must appeal to "outward signs" (as Moses did) or to traditional revelation such as the Bible. If the belief is

consistent with this, it is justified, but if not, it is enthusiasm and ought to
be rejected. Those who claim new truths without a sign and are led "con-
tinually round in this circle. *It is a revelation, because they firmly believe
it*, and *they believe it, because it is a revelation*" (*Essay.*: IV xix 9).

Recently there has been a revival of interest in religious experiences. It is useful to distinguish two questions about them: what do
they show about God's nature, if anything; and are those who undergo
them rational in thinking God is communicating with them?

In connection with the first question, one might argue that the prev-
alence of religious experiences in which people report a benevolent
God is evidence that there is such a being. Seen in this light, religious
experience is similar to experimental phenomena in science (such as
the refraction of light) which call for explanation. The result is a causal
argument for God's existence: religious experience is a phenomenon
best explained by positing a benevolent God.

But this argument is weak. As William James (1961: 333–4) pointed
out, the experiences are not uniformly positive. There is also a phenomenon of *diabolical mysticism*, in which mystics experience the superior being as dreadful and evil, and undergo terror and suffering, not
peace and tranquillity. James concludes that religious experiences do
not support a theistic world view over a non-theistic one, since similar
experiences that support contradictory hypotheses do not favour one
over the other.

The second question is more interesting. While admitting that religious experiences do not provide good evidence for God's existence, William Alston (1991: ch. 5) has recently argued that it is still rational for those who experience them to take them as providing divine guidance. He holds that the practice of religious experience is analogous to ordinary perceptual experience, and just as it is rational to trust perception, so it is rational for subjects to trust reports based on religious experience. Both presuppose a background of beliefs within which they are interpreted, a background that cannot be justified non-circularly and both result in *prima facie* justified beliefs, that is, beliefs that are justified so long as they are not overridden by conditions the practice recognizes as defeating circumstances. In the case of perception, the background is our common-sense theory of the conditions under which perception yields justified beliefs while, in the case of religious experience, it is the religious practice within which the experience takes place. For instance, a religious experience that contradicts central claims of the religious community in which it occurs is unjustified just as a perceptual belief formed in poor lighting or while you are under the influence of drugs is unjustified. The conclusion Alston draws is that there is no good reason to reject the practice of religious experience as irrational. If the same conditions hold for both, intellectual honesty requires that we either reject both or accept both.

This theory raises questions that cannot be examined here. But it should be noted that Alston's conclusion is quite limited. Religious experiences do not show that God exists, but presuppose it since they have to occur within a religious tradition. At best, they show the practitioners what to do or not do on specific occasions. Alston is aware of this. His aim is only to show that the practice is not irrational, as many non-believers charge. This raises issues about the nature of rationality and its relation to justification and knowledge, but they cannot be pursued here.

Summary

In this chapter, we have discussed some of the ways in which empiricism has affected the discussion of religious belief:

- Paley's empirical defence of the argument from design and Hume's objections;
- the role of Darwin's theory of natural selection in challenging the

claim that chance cannot explain the leading instances of design, such as the complexity of the eye;

- Locke's attempt to defend the rationality of faith by appeal to God's veracity and miracles;
- Hume's criticism of the rationality of belief in miracles and the two major interpretations of it;
- the nature and status of religious experience in justifying claims about the divine and his intentions.

conclusion

Naturalism and empiricism

We have seen that empiricism holds two theses: all ideas and beliefs are acquired; and all knowledge of real existence rests on experience. The first is an alternative to Descartes's innatism and the second a claim about the source of evidence about reality. The first three chapters focused on the major historical empiricists: Locke, Berkeley and Hume. We discussed Locke's defence of both theses and evaluated some of Leibniz's criticisms of his rejection of innatism. Descartes and Locke were reacting against the Aristotelian-medieval conception of science in light of the new science initiated by Galileo, Descartes himself and the English scientists, Newton and Boyle. In Chapter 2, we discussed Berkeley's claim that Locke's physical realism leads to skepticism and has to be replaced by a radically new metaphysics, idealism or what he labelled immaterialism. Much of the discussion centred on his criticisms of Locke and so was an extension of Chapter 1. The chapter on Hume sketched his attempt to elaborate Locke's theory of ideas as the foundation of a new science of human nature in his early book, *A Treatise of Human Nature*, but focused on his more strictly epistemological work, *An Enquiry Concerning Human Understanding*. We considered his defence of empiricism's second thesis in terms of his distinction between relations of ideas and matters of fact, his argument that induction cannot be justified non-circularly but must be assumed to be reliable and his theory of the nature of causation.

In the second part of the book, we explained the later development of empiricism by considering three of the problems it must deal with: the nature of knowledge from experience; the problem of explaining mathematical and logical knowledge, that is, the *a priori*; and its responses to rationalist charges that it leads to skepticism. In Chapter 4, we examined Sellars's rejection of the given and defended the reliabilist theory of perceptual knowledge against his view that the only defensible alternative to the given is a coherence theory of justification. Chapter 5 explained Locke's theory that mathematical and logical principles are *a priori* but not about real existence and the more radical theories of Mill, Peirce and Quine that the idea of the *a priori* is itself a mistake. In Chapter 6, we explained the main skeptical challenges facing empiricism: the problem of justifying beliefs about eternal reality and the basic sources of evidence, that is, perception, memory and induction. Finally, in Chapter 7, we examined the application of empiricism to religious belief, discussing the argument from design, faith and miracles and, more briefly, religious experience.

In conclusion, let us consider empiricism more generally and its implications for our understanding of ourselves in relation to the world. Descartes and Locke have divergent views of our relation to nature. Descartes posits an intellect that is the source of innate principles and science and cannot be explained by natural causes, but derives directly from God by a special creation in each of us. He holds that the imagination is part of the body and includes the power to receive and store images from perception, while the intellect is an immaterial substance with innate ideas and knowledge independent of associations made by the imagination. Furthermore, he holds that animals inferior to human beings have imagination and are capable of thinking to the extent that they can learn from experience and respond to stimuli, but they do not have intellects. The result is that he thinks human knowledge is based on a separate substance that views events in the body from a special vantage point analogous to the way in which God views natural events. Locke's only concessions to this are (i) that the mind may be a separate substance and (ii) that it has the power to justify propositions based on abstract ideas (which are fictions) *a priori*. We differ from the other animals in that we have the power of abstraction but, as with them, all our knowledge derives from interaction with nature. The result is that Locke thinks we are part of nature in a way in which we are not, according to Descartes.

Later empiricists tend to naturalize our cognitive faculties even further. Although we did not discuss it here, this is true even of Berkeley. He argues that we do not directly perceive distance, as introspection suggests, but judge it on the basis of visual cues and tactual sensations. He does not take introspection at face value, but explains it by positing unconscious inferences. He also agrees with Locke that human beings are closer to the brutes in intellectual capacities, although it is not clear whether this is consistent with his idealism. (He does not discuss the extent to which animals think, for example.)

The most influential empiricist, so far as the contemporary discussion is concerned, is Hume. Following Berkeley's lead, he argues that human reasoning is continuous with animal association. He also argues that we cannot show that we have knowledge in a way that will "satisfy our reason", and is a forerunner of reliabilism and externalism. Further, his arguments against religious knowledge continue to be discussed. Later empiricists echo these tendencies. Peirce, for example, held that, along with the theses that "all knowledge is based on experience" and that experiment is the only way to advance science, "we have to place this other equally important truth, that all human knowledge, up to the highest flights of science, is but the development of our inborn animal instincts" (Peirce 1955: 215).

These tendencies are attempts to naturalize knowledge. Naturalism in this sense attempts to explain phenomena without appeal to the supernatural, that is, it holds that nature is a closed causal system. This is a minimal sense of the term consistent with theism (which holds that nature has an external cause even though the events in it do not). It also does not imply materialism and is consistent with mind–body dualism. Locke and Hume are naturalists in this sense while Berkeley is not (since he holds that God forces real-thing ideas on us). But all empiricists explain knowledge of reality in naturalistic terms.

Quine goes even further and argues that we have to give up normative epistemology along with Descartes's idea of an external viewpoint. He holds that the only evidence a person has about the world depends on "the stimulation of his sensory receptors" and we cannot deduce our theory of the world from observations. Furthermore, we cannot appeal to psychology or biology since they are sciences and the result would be circularity. But, Quine argues, this is a problem only if our goal is to justify knowledge along Cartesian lines. It does not arise if we only want "to understand the link between observation and science". A naturalistic worldview takes philosophy to be continuous with science and not as "an a priori propaedeutic or groundwork for science" (Quine 1969a: 76; 1969b: 126).

This is a major challenge for empiricism, but Quine's view is not the only one. There are at least two other responses. First, as we saw, Sellars holds that we must reject foundationalism and understand rationality in terms of coherence. He does not think empiricism can simply assume the reliability of the basic sources – as "the thermometer view" does. If I interpret him correctly, his coherentism is not a rejection of empiricism (as some contemporary rationalists argue), but a theory of the role of normativity in the theory of knowledge. Rationality is not based on an independent faculty, but on our natural ability to reflect on ourselves and our relation to the environment. Secondly, there is also a reliabilist response that derives from Hume. As I argued above in § "Empiricism and common sense" (p. 133), Hume holds that justification rests on assumptions we cannot justify non-circularly, that is, on an externalist theory of rationality. According to this, our task as rational beings is to justify our beliefs and more advanced methods in terms of the three basic ones: perception, memory and induction, which must be assumed to be reliable. This is a partial concession to skepticism, since it admits that we cannot show that we have knowledge, but it does not mean that the empiricist must deny knowledge or relinquish the notion of "just reasoning". I briefly defended Hume's view on this question (in § "Empiricism and common sense" (p. 133)), but a fuller discussion is beyond the scope of the present work.

Questions for discussion and revision

introduction Empiricism and rationalism

1. Explain the distinction between the two senses of empiricism.
2. Explain the distinction between real existence and ideal existence. What does an empiricist have to hold about mathematical propositions such as "Parallel lines never meet"? People sometimes say that God exists in our minds. Is this a form of belief in God?
3. What is a synthetic *a priori* proposition?
4. In what sense is a hallucination dependent on mind? Give an example.

one Locke, knowledge and the innate

1. How did the new science undermine the Aristotelian-medieval theory? How do Descartes and Locke try to solve the problem?
2. What are Leibniz's main criticisms of Locke's attack on innatism? To what extent does he misrepresent Locke's position? What is the main issue between them?
3. Explain Locke's theory of natural science. To what extent does he think we can discover the ultimate nature of things? To what extent is he skeptical?
4. What does Locke mean by "sensitive knowledge"? How does he defend its claim to be knowledge? What problems does it pose for him?

two Berkeley's idealism

1. Explain and evaluate Berkeley's main argument for idealism.

2. Explain idealism and realism. Does Berkeley's version of it reduce the world to illusion? Discuss.
3. Why does Berkeley's idealism seem inconsistent with his empiricism? Is the charge just? Why does it seem to assume the existence of God? Does it?
4. What is the relation between Berkeley's idealism and his criticism of Locke's doctrine of abstraction? Does Locke's theory allow the realist to show that we can conceive of something existing unconceived?
5. Explain Locke's theories of substance and the primary–secondary quality distinction and Berkeley's objections.

three Induction and Hume's empiricism

1. Explain Hume's distinction between the types of propositions and its relation to his statement of empiricism. What is his argument for empiricism?
2. Explain the problem of induction and Hume's "skeptical solution". In what sense is it a solution?
3. Explain Hume's two definitions of cause. Which is more basic? Do they imply that causation is an illusion?
4. Explain the debate over the New Hume.
5. What is Hume's theory of belief? What problems does it give rise to? Can they be avoided?

four Empiricism and foundations

1. What problem is the foundations theory meant to address? Discuss the alternatives to it and their prospects.
2. What does Sellars understand by the theory of the given? Explain and evaluate the arguments against it.
3. In what way is the debate over the theory of the given similar to that over innate knowledge?
4. Explain the difference between coherence and reliabilist theories of justification. What are some of the objections to them?

five Empiricism and the *a priori*

1. Explain the distinctions between necessary and contingent propositions, and empirical and *a priori* propositions.
2. Explain Kant's theory of the analytic–synthetic distinction and the problem with it. How does Frege propose to deal with it?
3. To what extent are the views of Peirce and Quine on the *a priori* extensions of Mill's?
4. What problem does mathematical knowledge pose for empiricism? What is

the common thread if any in the theories of Locke, Mill, Peirce and Quine? How do they differ?

5. Explain and evaluate the main objections to the notion of *a priori* justification.

six Empiricism and skepticism

1. Explain the distinction between knowledge and knowledge with certainty. To what extent does the distinction clarify the question of skepticism?
2. Explain the problem of the external world. To what extent is it a problem for representative realism, idealism and direct realism?
3. What is the veil-of-perception problem? How might the representative realist deal with it? How might the phenomenalist deal with it?
4. Explain the problem of justifying the sources of knowledge and the ways in which rationalists and empiricists have dealt with it. Can the problem be solved? If not, what are the implications for our conception of knowledge?
5. Explain Goodman's "new riddle"? To what extent is it a new problem of induction?
6. Explain Moore's approach to the problem of skepticism. To what extent does it refute skepticism, if at all?

seven Empiricism and religious belief

1. Explain Paley's version of the argument from design. Why does he think chance cannot account for complexity? Are his arguments sound?
2. To what extent does Hume agree with Paley about the argument? What does he think its limitations are?
3. Explain Aquinas's and Locke's views on faith and reason. To what extent do they differ? Are their differences significant from a religious point of view?
4. Explain Hume's argument against miracles. What are the two interpretations of the argument?
5. What are religious experiences and do they support belief in God?

Further reading

introduction Empiricism and rationalism

For an introductory survey of empiricism and Locke, Berkeley and Hume, see Frederick Copleston, *A History of Philosophy* V, parts I and II (Garden City, NY: Image Books, 1964).

Good historical introductions to the empiricists and rationalists are R. S. Woolhouse, *The Empiricists* (Oxford: Oxford University Press, 1988), and John Cottingham, *The Rationalists* (Oxford: Oxford University Press, 1988).

For other treatments of empiricism, see Laurence BonJour, *Epistemology* (Lanham, MD: Rowman and Littlefield, 2002), ch. 5, and Thomas Nagel, *The View From Nowhere* (Oxford: Oxford University Press, 1986), ch. 5. For a defence of the view presented here, see R. G. Meyers, "Was Locke an Empiricist?", *Locke Studies* I (2001), 63–85. For Bertrand Russell's view of the question, see Bertrand Russell, *Problems of Philosophy* (Oxford: Oxford University Press, 1959), chs VII and VIII.

one Locke, knowledge and the innate

Locke's *Essay*, I ii–iv, contains Locke's famous discussion of innate knowledge. For Descartes's view, see *Meditations* II–III. Leibniz's criticisms are found in the Preface of *New Essays on Human Understanding*, 43–68. For an excellent discussion of the issue, see Robert Merrihew Adams, "Where do our Ideas come from: Descartes vs. Locke", in *Innate Ideas*, S. P. Stich (ed.), 71–87 (Berkeley, CA: University of California Press, 1975).

Useful books on Locke are: Nicholas Jolley, *Locke: His Philosophical Thought* (Oxford: Oxford University Press, 1999); Vere Chappell (ed.), *The Cambridge Companion to Locke* (Cambridge: Cambridge University Press, 1994); Michael Ayers,

Locke (London: Routledge, 1991); and J. L. Mackie, *Problems From Locke* (Oxford: Clarendon Press, 1976).

A pivotal work in Locke scholarship is Maurice Mandelbaum, "Locke's Realism", in his *Philosophy, Science and Sense Perception*, 1–60 (Baltimore, MD: Johns Hopkins University Press, 1964).

two Berkeley's idealism

General works are: J. O. Urmson, *Berkeley* (Oxford: Oxford University Press, 1982); D. M. Armstrong, "Introduction", in *Berkeley's Philosophical Writings*, D. M. Armstrong (ed.), 7–34 (New York: Collier, 1965); and Kenneth P. Winkler, *Berkeley: An Interpretation* (Oxford: Clarendon Press, 1989).

For Berkeley's criticisms of Locke, see Mandelbaum, "Locke's Realism". For criticisms of his master argument, see A. N. Prior, "Berkeley in Logical Form", in his *Papers in Logic and Ethics*, 33–8 (London: Duckworth, 1976), and J. L. Mackie, "Self-refutation: A Formal Analysis", *Philosophical Quarterly* **14** (1964), 193–203.

three Induction and Hume's empiricism

For a survey of Hume's views, see Copleston, *A History of Philosophy*, V, pt. II. Also useful are: A. J. Ayer, *Hume* (New York: Hill and Wang, 1980); Anthony Flew, *Hume's Theory of Belief* (New York: Humanities Press, 1961); and E. C. Mossner, *The Life of David Hume*, 2nd edn (Oxford: Clarendon Press, 1980).

For the current debate on Hume's theory of causation see: Rupert Read & K. A. Richman (eds), *The New Hume Debate* (London: Routledge, 2000); Galen Strawson, *The Secret Connexion: Causation, Realism, and David Hume* (Oxford: Clarendon Press, 1989); Kenneth P. Winkler, "The New Hume", *Philosophical Review* **100** (1991), 541–79; and Tom L. Beauchamp (ed.), *Philosophical Problems of Causation* (Encino, CA: Dickenson, 1974), especially the articles by Ayer, Popper and Kneale.

four Empiricism and foundations

On the general problem of coherence, foundations and reliabilism, see: Russell, *Problems of Philosophy*, chs V, XIII; R. G. Meyers, *The Likelihood of Knowledge* (Dordrecht: Kluwer, 1988), chs 6, 7; Laurence BonJour, *The Structure of Empirical Knowledge* (Cambridge, MA: Harvard University Press, 1985); and Alvin Goldman, "What Is Justified Belief?", in *Naturalizing Epistemology*, H. Kornblith (ed.) (Cambridge, MA: MIT Press, 1987). The last is also reproduced in other anthologies of epistemology.

On Sellars's theory, see R. G. Meyers, "Sellars' Rejection of Foundations", *Philosophical Studies* **39** (1981), 61–78, and Willem A. DeVries & Timm Triplet, *Knowlege, Mind and the Given* (Indianapolis, IN: Hackett, 2000). A detailed defence of the given can be found in H. H. Price, *Perception*, 2nd edn (London: Methuen, 1950). For a discussion of "the introspective method," see *Examination*: ch. XI.

five Empiricism and the *a priori*

For defences of rationalism, see: Russell, *Problems of Philosophy*, chs VIII–X; A. C. Ewing, *The Fundamental Questions of Philosophy* (New York: Collier, 1962), ch. 2; and Laurence BonJour, *In Defence of Pure Reason* (Cambridge: Cambridge University Press, 1998).

For Mill's views, see *System*: II iv–vi. Frege's criticisms are in *The Foundations of Arithmetic*, J. L. Austin (trans.) (New York: Harper, 1960), §§7–10. See also Anthony Kenny, *Frege* (Harmondsworth: Penquin, 1995). For an evaluation, see Glenn Kessler, "Frege, Mill, and the Foundations of Arithmetic", *Journal of Philosophy* **76** (1980), 65–79. The defence of Mill in the text draws heavily on John Skorupski, *John Stuart Mill* (London: Routledge, 1989).

C. S. Peirce, *Philosophical Writings*, J. Buchler (ed.) (New York: Dover, 1955), ch. 11, contains his theory of inference. Quine's views are defended in "Two Dogmas of Empiricism", in *From a Logical Point of View*, 2nd edn, 20–46 (New York: Harper, 1961).

six Empiricism and skepticism

For Hume's views, see *Treatise*: I iv 7, and *EHU*: XII. A good introduction to the problem is Russell, *Problems of Philosophy*, chs I–III, VI. An excellent discussion of the veil of perception can be found in Mackie, *Problems From Locke*, ch. 2. On phenomenalism and skepticism, see A. J. Ayer, *The Problem of Knowledge* (Harmondsworth: Penguin, 1956), ch. 2. Ayer's views are criticized by J. L. Austin, in *Sense and Sensibilia* (Oxford: Oxford University Press, 1964), esp. 45–54.

For a succinct (and inflential) discussion of sources of knowledge and skepticism, see Roderick M. Chisholm, *Theory of Knowledge* (Englewood Cliffs, NJ: Prentice-Hall, 1966), ch. 4.

Meyers, *The Likelihood of Knowledge*, ch. 8, defends a reliabilist–externalist approach to the question. G. Santayana, *Scepticism and Animal Faith* (New York: Dover, 1959), defends scepticism.

seven Empiricism and religious belief

Classic works on the argument from design are Hume's *Dialogues Concerning Natural Religion* (*DNR*) and W. Paley, *Natural Theology: Selections* (Indianapolis, IN: Bobbs-Merrill, 1963). J. Hick, *The Philosophy of Religion*, 3rd edn (Englewood Cliffs, NJ: Prentice-Hall, 1983), ch. 2, is a clear, introductory discussion. See also Brian Davies, *An Introduction to the Philosophy of Religion* (Oxford: Oxford University Press, 1982).

On the problem of faith and the role of miracles see Locke's *Essay*: IV xviii–xix, and T. Aquinas, *On Faith and Reason*, S. F. Brown (ed.) (Indianapolis, IN: Hackett, 1999), esp. pt I. For modern discussions, see Richard Swinburne, *The Concept of Miracle* (Basingstoke: Macmillan, 1970) and his edited collection *Miracles* (Basingstoke: Macmillan, 1989). For a defence of Hume on miracles, see R. G. Meyers, "The Marvelous and Miraculous: A Defense of Hume", http://rgm95.tripod.com/homepage/id5.html (accessed June 2006).

For a classic discussion of religious experience, W. James, *Varieties of Religious Experience* (New York: Collier, 1961), lectures 16, 17. W. Alston, *Perceiving God* (Ithaca, NY: Cornell University Press, 1991) offers a limited defence within the context of contemporary theory of knowledge.

A useful collection on religious knowledge is Louis P. Pojman (ed.), *Philosophy of Religion* (Belmont, CA: Wadsworth, 2003).

conclusion Naturalism and empiricism

Kornblith, *Naturalizing Epistemology*, contains Quine's "Epistemology Naturalized" and "Natural Kinds", as well as other papers on the issue.

References

Alston, W. 1991. *Perceiving God*. Ithaca, NY: Cornell University Press.

Aquinas, T. 1999. *On Faith and Reason*, S. F. Brown (ed.). Indianapolis, IN: Hackett.

Austin, J. L. 1962. *Sense and Sensibilia*. Oxford: Oxford University Press.

Berkeley, G. 1993. *Alciphron: In Focus*, David Berman (ed.). London: Routledge.

BonJour, L. 2000. "Can Empirical Knowledge Have a Foundation?". In *Epistemology: An Anthology*, E. Sosa & J. Kim (eds), 261–73. Oxford: Blackwell.

Brentano, F. 1969. *The Origin of Our Knowledge of Right and Wrong*, R. M. Chisholm & E. H. Schneewind (trans.). London: Routledge.

Copleston, F. 1964. *A History of Philosophy V*. Garden City, NY: Image Books..

Ewing, A. C. 1962. *The Fundamental Questions of Philosophy*. New York: Collier.

Frege, G. 1960. *The Foundations of Arithmetic*, J. L. Austin (trans.). New York: Harper.

Goodman, N. 1955. "The New Riddle of Induction". In *Fact, Fiction, and Forecast*, 63–86. Cambridge, MA: Harvard University Press.

Hamilton, W. 1877. *Metaphysics*, F. Bowen (ed.) Boston: Allyn.

Hick, J. 1983. *The Philosophy of Religion*, 3rd edn. Englewood Cliffs, NJ: Prentice-Hall.

James, W. 1961. *Varieties of Religious Experience*. New York: Collier.

Leibniz, G. W. 1981. *New Esssays on Human Understanding*, Peter Tremnant & Jonathan Bennett (eds). Cambridge: Cambridge University Press.

Locke, J. 1972. "Deus". In Lord King, *The Life and Letters of John Locke*, 313–16. New York, 1972. Originally published in 1829.

Moore, G. E. 1959. "Hume's Philosophy." In *Philosophical Studies*, 147–67. Paterson, NJ: Littlefield, Adams.

Mossner, E. C. 2001. *The Life of David Hume*, 2nd edn. Oxford: Oxford University Press.

Paley, W. 1963. *Natural Theology: Selections*. Indianapolis, IN: Bobbs-Merrill.

Peirce, C. S. 1955. *Philosophical Writings*, Justus Buchler (ed.). New York: Dover.

Popper, K. R. 1968. *The Logic of Scientific Discovery*. New York: Harper.

Price, H. H. 1950. *Perception*, 2nd edn. London: Methuen.

Quine, W. V. 1961. "Two Dogmas of Empiricism". In *From a Logical Point of View*, 2nd edn, 20–46. New York: Harper.

Quine, W. V. 1969a. "Epistemology Naturalized". In *Ontological Relativity and Other Essays*, 69–90. New York: Columbia University Press.

Quine, W. V. 1969b. "Natural Kinds". In *Ontological Relativity and Other Essays*, 114–38. New York: Columbia University Press.

Russell, B. 1959. *Problems of Philosophy*. Oxford: Oxford University Press.

Santayana, G. 1955. *Scepticism and Animal Faith*. New York: Dover.

Sellars, W. 1963. "Empiricism and the Philosophy of Mind". In *Science, Perception, and Reality*, 127–96. London: Routledge.

Sellars, W. 1975. Epistemic Principles". In *Action, Knowledge and Reality*, H. N. Casteñeda (ed.), 332–46. Indianapolis, IN: Bobbs-Merrill.

Index